Basic Scenery for Model Railroaders

The Complete P

Lou Sassi

KALMBACH
BOOKS

Contents

Printed in the United States of America

03 04 05 06 07 08 09   10 9 8 7 6 5 4 3 2

Visit our website at http://kalmbachbooks.com
Secure online ordering available

Publisher's Cataloging-in-Publication
(Provided by Quality Books, Inc.)

Sassi, Lou.
    Basic scenery for model railroaders / Lou Sassi. —
1st ed.
    p. cm.
    ISBN: 0-89024-422-7
  I. Title

TF197.S27 2001   625.1'9
            QBI01-201090

    1. Railroads—Models. 2. Miniature craft.

Art director: Kristi Ludwig
Book design: Sabine Beaupré

Rural Landscape

Roads

Details

⏱ *symbol indicates a one-evening project that can easily be completed in the course of an evening or any other time you have a few hours to work on your model railroad.*

Acknowledgments

I would like to thank the following people and manufacturers for helping make this book possible: Lee Karakas from Woodland Scenics, Scott Grubbs from Homabed, Jack LaRussa from NJ International, Larry Galler from C.S. Designs Inc., Dale Rush from Blair Line, Don Tichy from Creative Model Associates, Gregg Scott and Jim Moffet from G.H.Q., Jim Elster from Scenic Express, Bob and Ron Rands from Micro Engineering, Tony Parisi from Tony's Train Xchange, the folks at Activa Products, Alder Models, AMSI, Grandt Line, and Kent Johnson, from Kalmbach Publishing Co.

A special thanks also to Mark Pendergrass from the Norton Company, whose buffing pads allowed my evergreen forests to flourish, Bruce Sparrow from Precision Laser Craft for supplying me with his excellent self-stick roof shingles, Rich Cobb from O&W Shops, perhaps the finest scratchbuilder in the Northeast, and my good friends Pete Darling and Bert Sacco, who have given, unselfishly, of their time and talent.

As always, I must say thank you to my wife, Cheryl, without whose knowledge and guidance this book would not have been possible.

—Lou Sassi

In the Beginning

I was introduced to scale model railroading one chilly day in December of 1958. It was noon hour, and I was on a break from classes at Saratoga Springs High School, where I was a freshman. As I surveyed the shelves of the local news-stand for something to read, I caught a glimpse of the cover of a magazine called *Model Railroader*. Picking up the book and leafing through the pages, I came across a layout story about the HO scale Texas Rio Grande & Western Railroad written by Bill McClanahan. A few pages later I found a section called "Trackside Photos." I was particularly impressed by the photos of a Shay crossing a spindly trestle (built by Cliff Grandt) and a three-quarter view of a steam locomotive spotted at a freight house (built by Jack Work). I was amazed at how the detailed structures and scenery brought the model trains to life.

Wata Idea

Pan ahead to 1982. After years of experimenting with plaster, sawdust, and all sorts of concoctions in pursuit of the creation of my miniature hills and dales, I happened upon a book, *How to Build Realistic Model Railroad Scenery,* by a couple of fellows named Dave Frary and Bob Hayden. I was again amazed. Here were two guys that actually went out into the woods and fields by their homes and found the raw materials of "real" scenery with which to make model scenery. They used lichen for trees and dirt to make DIRT! All this stuff was affixed to the layout using white glue and water.

In the Nick-a-Time

It was very fortunate that Dave and Bob chose to write their book when they did because it corresponded to the time I seriously started construction of my first (and present) miniature railroad empire. Since then, my scenery techniques have been influenced and altered by a number of other people. An article in *Model Railroader* in the 1980s introduced plaster gauze (the stuff they wrap broken arms and legs in) as a scenery base. A fellow named Ken Osen decided to share his ideas about scenery at a number of NMRA National Conventions. I was sure to be in the front row at every one of them. Among other things, he introduced me to such ideas as furnace-filter-and-sphagnum-moss evergreen trees, peppergrass hardwoods, tea-leaf "dead" leaves, and most important, a concoction called "Ground Goop."

A Bird in the Hand

After a number of years experimenting with the ideas and techniques I had learned from these folks, I was contacted by fellow modeler Bob Hamm. Bob had met two fellows at a local round-robin train group that were experimenting with their own scenery techniques. Knowing my interest in the subject, Bob thought it might fun if the four of us got together and started sharing our ideas. I agreed, and the resulting "Tree Group" became one of the most enjoyable, informative groups I had ever been involved with. Some of the fruits of those (Wednesday night) meetings were shared with our fellow modelers in the May, July, September, and November 1995 issues of *Model Railroader* Magazine.

Einstein I'm Not

As you may have surmised by now, the projects that follow are a collection of techniques I have learned over the years. I will be the first to admit that I am not ingenious enough to have invented them all myself. Many have been culled from the work of others.

So I suppose you can look at this book as a conglomeration of some of my own ideas along with those of others that I have used in their original form or altered to suit my needs. Most of them were used to prepare the West Hoosic Division for its appearance in Allen's *Great Model Railroads Video no. 23* and Kalmbach's annual *Great Model Railroads* publication. I believe all of them are worthy of your consideration as a viable means to an end—

that end being realistic miniature scenery.

There is one particularly important observation that you must bear in mind if your miniature scenery is going to look believable. After studying the woods and fields in my area firsthand, I have noticed that foliage—be it grass, bushes, or trees—has a constant base hue that ties everything together, regardless of variations in color. This is as true anywhere in the country as it is in the Northeast, and it is not that difficult to replicate. Just like Mother Nature, we have to make our colors blend. This blending of colors will take place as you follow the projects in this book. Although the products used for each project range from natural to manmade (many by different manufacturers), I have made sure they are color-compatible.

Enuff Already

Enough philosophy. Let's get to work . . . or play, if you wish. I hope you enjoy tackling this series of projects as much as I've enjoyed preparing them for you. Happy model railroading!

Foaming at the Base

A lightweight alternative to a hardshell scenery base

Tools List

Woodland Scenics
Subterrain System:
  Foam Knife, ST1433
  Foam Knife Blades,
    ST1434
  Foam Pencils, ST1431
  Low-Temp Foam Glue
    Gun, ST1445

Hot-Wire Foam
  Cutter, ST1435
Putty knife
Ruler
NMRA track gauge
Saber saw
Phillips screwdriver

After years of building layout framework out of saber-saw-cut plywood supported by risers and frame members made from dimensional (one-by) lumber, I longed for an alternative that was easier to work with and possibly lighter. In the past I had experimented with blue and gray extruded foam (the kind used for home insulation) as a scenery base. Unfortunately, its advantages—light weight and compatibility with water-soluble scenery techniques—were offset by a number of disadvantages. Rasping the material with a Surform file created thousands of electrostatically

While shuttling that B&M boxcar, the boys got a little rough and dropped a whole container of Styrofoam sheets on the main. They better clean it up in a hurry—there will be a freight through soon.

charged particles that seemed to stick to anything within a hundred yards of the project. Just when it looked like all hope was lost, I happened upon a Woodland Scenics Subterrain System, as they call it, consisting of high-density foam sheets, risers, inclines, and profile boards of various thickness. They also supply all the materials and tools necessary to attach the foam

Materials List

Woodland Scenics
Subterrain System:
  Assorted thickness
    foam sheets
  Assorted thickness
    foam risers
  Assorted thickness
    foam inclines
Foam Putty, ST1447
Foam Tack Glue,
  ST1444

Foam Nails, ST1432
Low-Temp Glue
  Sticks, ST1446
Homabed roadbed
Masking tape
No. 6 x ¾″ flathead
wood screws
(1) 4 x 8-foot sheet of
tempered Masonite

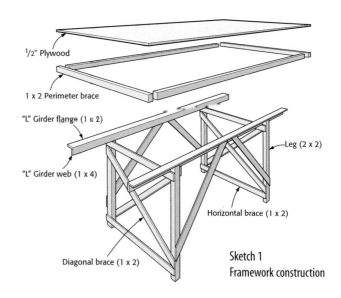

1/2″ Plywood

1 x 2 Perimeter brace

"L" Girder flange (1 x 2)

"L" Girder web (1 x 4)

Diagonal brace (1 x 2)

Leg (2 x 2)

Horizontal brace (1 x 2)

Sketch 1
Framework construction

The finished layout base, L girders, 1″ x 2″ perimeter bracing, and leg assemblies.

to the layout base and carve the foam to the desired contours. There are a number of advantages to their system. First, just like its home-improvement brother, the foam is very lightweight. Second, it is designed to be built upon any rigid, flat, surface. This eliminates having to build wooden open grid-work, risers, and saber-sawed plywood trackbed. Most important, the Woodland Scenics foam does not emit toxic fumes when cut with a hot-wire cutter.

A number of the projects in this book were to be built on a 6 x 2-foot diorama that I hoped to make as portable, and therefore as lightweight, as possible. So it seemed like the ideal time to experiment with the new Woodland Scenics system. After reading their manual a couple of

times, I ordered the Sub-terrain video (ST1401) to get an even better idea of the process. With both of these sources of information under my belt, I decided it was time to put the system to the test. I started by cutting a ½″ sheet of plywood to 2½ x 6 feet for a base. I made up a pair of 6-foot long (1″ x 2″ over 1″ x 4″) L gird-ers, which I mounted to the bottom of the plywood 15″ apart. Although you could use a set of commercially available folding legs if you prefer, I chose to make up a

set of 2″ x 2″ legs cross-braced with 1″ x 2″ diago-nals for rigidity. After attach-ing them to the L girders, I added diagonal long braces. Since I planned to add a ⅛″ Masonite fascia later, I attached strips of 1″ x 2″ stock around the bottom perimeter of the plywood. Then I could attach the fas-cia to solid pine rather than the laminated edge of the ½″-thick sheet of plywood. The sketch above shows the indi-vidual component assembly, and the photo at top shows the finished product.

9

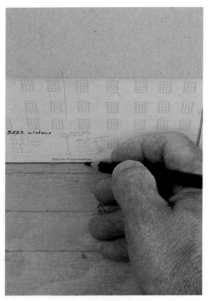

1 After gathering all the necessary materials and tools, I laid out the track plan on the plywood by marking the track center line. I then measured 1¼" on either side of the center line and drew two more lines parallel to it. This marked the outside edge of the Homabed track bed.

2 I used cardboard mockups of the proposed buildings to test them for size and visual impact. After checking track clearances with an NMRA gauge, I drew lines around the mockups to mark their location on the plywood base

3 When I was satisfied with the location of all the components, I pinned the foam risers in place with Foam Nails and then later ran a bead of Low-Temp Foam Glue around their base with the glue gun.

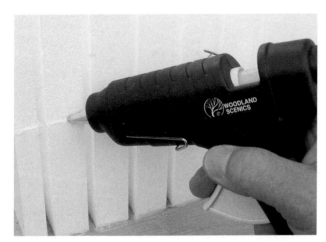

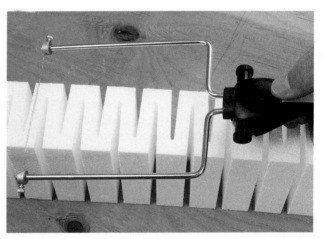

4 Since I wanted 8" of vertical drop from track level to the lowest ground level (the bottom of a waterfall and cascading stream) I stacked two 4"-high risers on top of one another. After pinning them together, I attached each stacked section to the one below it with a bead of hot glue.

5 I wanted the siding to Peerless Leather to be at a slightly lower grade than the mainline trackage, so I used risers of different thicknesses to achieve this effect. After marking the correct (siding) length on each riser with the foam marker, I cut each one with the hot-wire cutter.

6 I stacked the risers, piece of incline, and a section of ¼" sheet stock to arrive at an elevation about ⅛" lower than the main line and hot-glued them together.

7 Once the trackwork support foam was in place, it was time to attach the surrounding ground support foam panels. It's only necessary to have solid panels from ground level up. I started with the millpond base and the hillside to the left of it. I first cut some blocks of 4"-thick stock and attached them to the plywood with the hot-glue gun.

8 Next, I applied some hot glue to the blocks and attached a solid 4"-thick block as a base for the hillside and a 3"-thick block as a base for the millpond. This would make the pond elevation at least 1" lower than the surrounding area.

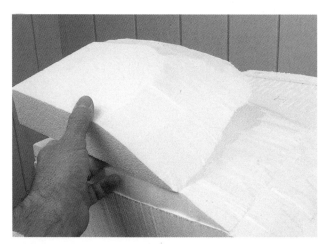

9 On one end of the pond I planned a hillside sloping upward to the edge of the layout. This was created by cutting individual panels of various thicknesses of foam to form a gradual slope.

10 I used some of the remnant material to provide sloping ground along the edge of the pond at the fascia.

Before You Continue …

At this stage of construction you must decide what you are going to use for "water" in the pond and stream bed. If you use Envirotex, as I did, you must protect the surface of the foam. (Although Envirotex is solid when cured, it is applied as a liquid.) If you don't protect the surface, the Envirotex will eat through the foam and you will have a miniature open pit mine instead of a pond. You can seal the pond base, sides, and stream bed with a couple of layers of plaster cloth, or do as I did, and cut a piece of ⅛"-thick Masonite to fit between the foam and the Envirotex pond water. If you choose the latter method, the Masonite must fit under the final layers of foam that form the perimeter of the pond—so do not attach them permanently at this time. Refer to the project "Down by the Old Mill Stream" for particulars.

11 With the pond base and hillside finished, I turned my attention to the dam and cascading waterfall. I developed this by cutting and fitting various thicknesses of foam (using the hot wire) to create a series of three falls that would carry the water from the dam, around a curve, beneath the track, and off the layout. I used Foam Nails to hold everything in place until I had test-fitted the entire area. Once the pond and waterfall areas were done, I built up the foam on the opposite side of the stream to form a flat base for a farm scene.

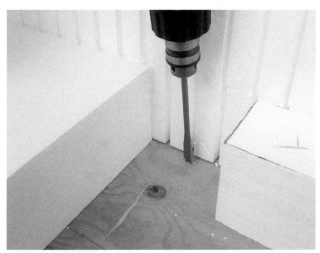

12 Before adding the finished solid foam panels along the track opposite the mill and farm, I installed track feeder wires. I first drilled a hole through the plywood base with a ½"-diameter drill bit.

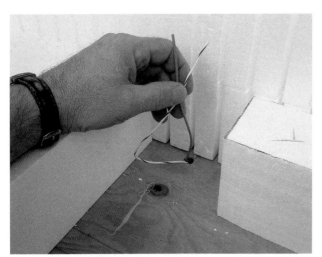

13 I fed the wires through the hole and tied them off so they could be soldered to the rails later.

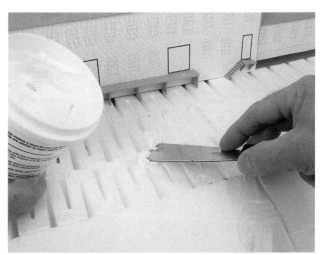

14 With all of the foam work done, it was time to fill any voids in the material and add roadbed. Since I planned to add track roadbed directly to the risers and not cover them with plaster gauze (as Woodland Scenics suggests doing), I decided to fill the gaps in the risers with Foam Putty. Foam Putty looks like spackling compound but is much less dense and applies easily with a putty knife.

15 Once the Foam Putty had dried, I applied some Foam Tack Glue to the surface of the risers and pressed Homabed roadbed strips in place.

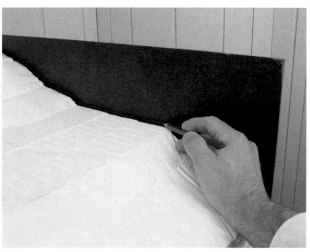

16 I chose to use ⅛"-thick tempered Masonite for the fascia panels. After carefully measuring the length of each side of the module, I cut four panels from a 4 x 8-foot sheet of Masonite. While I was careful to make the length of each panel exact, I allowed plenty of excess width. I temporarily attached each panel to the module by screwing no. 6 wood screws into the 1" x 2" furring strips that I attached to the bottom of the plywood base earlier (sketch 1). I marked the ground (foam) contours along the top edge of each panel with a foam marking pencil. I removed the panels and cut along the contour lines with a saber saw.

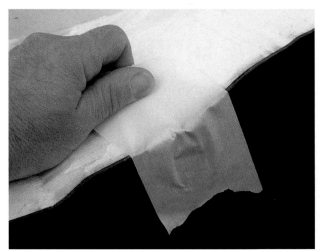

17 After applying a bead of Foam Tack Glue along the top edge of the foam contour sheets, I remounted the Masonite panels permanently, using masking tape to temporarily hold them in place along their top edges until the glue dried.

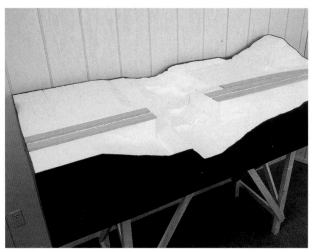

18 The finished Subterrain layout awaits final scenicking.

Covering Some Ground

A simple technique to cover unscenicked areas

Tools List

Fine-, medium-, and
coarse-mesh kitchen
sieves
Magnet
Small paintbrush
Artist's spatula

Spoon
Eyedroppers
Spray bottle
Rave Mega Hold
hairspray

Because of America's agri-cultural heritage, much of our rural countryside consists of cleared but uncul-tivated farm fields. Using a combination of natural and commercial materials, it is quite simple for a modeler to replicate these open fields in miniature. Just bear in mind that, as always, variety of tex-ture and color is the secret to good-looking scenery.

The primary natural mate-rial required for an open field is plain old dirt. Medium to dark browns and grays work best. Stay away from anything containing clay. Mixing a clay-based soil with water will result in a slimy mess. You also don't

Boston & Maine RS-3 no. 1507 rolls past Peerless Leather Company as it heads east out of Shelburne Falls towards Greenfield, Massachusetts. This project explains how to make the field in the foreground.

want to use anything with magnetic particles in it. Passing a magnet over your dirt will help you determine if this is a problem. Once I'm sure my dirt is nonmagnetic, I like to run it through a number of progressively finer mesh kitchen sieves and categorize the results in Tupperware containers. This way I can control the tex-ture of the material during application. Another natural

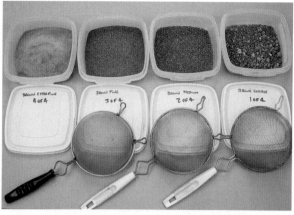

Materials List

Nonmagnetic dirt
Tea leaves
AMSI:
    Spring Green foam
      (fine), 401
    Spring Green foam
      (coarse), 402
    Yellow Green foam
      (fine), 411
    Yellow Green foam
      (coarse), 412
    Grass Green foam
      (fine), 441
    Grass Green foam
      (coarse), 442
    Groundcover
      material, 30001G
    Groundcover
      material, 30002G
Woodland Scenics:
    Blended Turf
      foam, 49
    Polyfiber mesh, 178

Permascene (JCS
Incorporated)
Celluclay (Activa
Products)
(1) gallon Elmer's Glue
All (white glue) (used
for Ground Goop mix
and 1:1 with water as
fixative for groundcover
materials)
(1) 12 oz. bottle Lysol
Concentrate
(1) gallon Pittsburgh
Tobacco Brown interior
flat latex paint, 7607
(1) quart "wet" water
(tap water with one or
two drops of dishwash-
ing liquid added

material I like to use is tea leaves. I pick up the cheapest variety I can find at the supermarket. These are spread over the ground at random to create the look of dead leaves. (Come to think about it . . . isn't that what they are?)

When it comes to commercial materials, our field will require an assortment of ground foams and polyfiber mesh. These will represent grass and weeds. My favorite "open field" ground foams are AMSI (Architectural Model Supply Inc.) Spring Green, Yellow Green, and

Grass Green. I also use Woodland Scenics Green Blended Turf. For higher brush, I sprinkle the finer grade foams over Woodland Scenics polyfiber mesh and AMSI fine and coarse groundcover material (also a fiber mesh).

I use a concoction called "Ground Goop" as a base for all my ground textures. This is a mix of 1 cup Celluclay, 1 cup Permascene*, 1 cup earth-colored latex paint (Pittsburgh Tobacco Brown), ½ cup white glue, and one capful of Lysol (concentrate) or similar disinfectant. The

Categorize dirt from very fine to coarse by running it through kitchen sieves.

Tea leaves make good dead-leaf groundcover.

The components of "Ground Goop": Permascene*, Celluclay, earth-color latex paint, Elmer's white glue, and Lysol concentrated disinfectant.

Lysol prevents mold buildup. I add enough water to this concoction to bring it to the consistency of peanut butter.

* Permascene is no longer available. I now use "New Era" vermiculite available at house & garden centers and hardware stores.

1 I find it best to brush-paint whatever base material I'm using with full-strength earth-color latex paint before applying Goop or foam. This will prevent any raw plaster, Styrofoam, or other material that is not earth-colored from showing through the final groundcover.

2 After the paint has fully dried, use an artist's spatula to apply a layer of Goop about 1/8" thick to a 1-foot-square area.

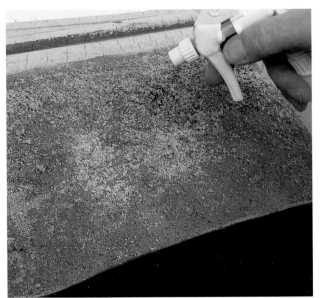

3 Next, sprinkle on different colors and textures of dirt, ground foam, and tea leaves.

4 When you're satisfied with the results, mist the entire area with "wet" water (tap water with a drop or two of dishwashing liquid added to increase capillary action).

5 Wetting the area will usually reveal spots where there may not be enough dirt or foam to completely cover the Goop. If that is the case (and it usually is), then spread more dirt and foam for thorough coverage.

6 Once these areas are rewet, finish by applying a white glue–water mix (1 part glue to 1 part water) to the entire area with an eyedropper.

7 After everything has dried, add larger polyfiber bushes. Do this by first pulling the polyfiber apart into small pieces about an inch square. You'll then pull each of these smaller pieces apart, spreading the material out to make it less dense.

8 Place the polyfiber on the ground, press it down with your fingers, and sprinkle fine-textured AMSI foam on its surface. Now fix the foam and the polyfiber in place with a spritz of pump-style hair spray.

Concocting a Conifer

Easy techniques for making evergreens

Rutland engine 208 with a freight drag at milepost 43 on the main line. The evergreens in the lower foreground were made with the materials and techniques described in this project.

Tools List

Scissors
Pocket knife
Pin vise

Razor saw
Small paintbrush

The conifer family of evergreens consists of the pine, larch, spruce, hemlock, Douglas fir, and fir. They are all roughly conical in shape and all but the larch hold their needles year round (hence the term evergreen). The last five varieties are very easily modeled. If you want a better idea of what the different types of conifers look like and where they grow, you might want to pick up a copy of *Trees of North America* by Alan Mitchell. For a more in-depth study of trees in general, the Textbook of Dendrology by Harlow and Harrar, published by McGraw-Hill, might be the answer.

After trying numerous materials and methods over the years, attempting to come up with a good-look-

Materials List

Bear-Tex:
   General-purpose
     pad, 74700
   Scouring pad, 79600
   Hand pad, 85100
Industrial scrubbing pad
Furnace filters
Quick Grab cement
AMSI Conifer Green
ground foam, 10451

Assorted bamboo
skewers
Pine, balsa, or basswood
stripwood
Floral wire
Minwax Special Walnut
stain, 224
Rave Mega Hold no. 4
hairspray
Brown spray paint

Spray the furnace filter with brown paint.

ing miniature evergreen tree, I came to the conclusion that the buffing pad / furnace filter variety seemed to yield the most believable conifer tree for the least amount of time and effort.

I found four types of buffing pads that work well. They are all made by the Norton Company and are available at most well-stocked hardware stores. If you can't find them there, or if you decide to buy in bulk, Norton Company's address and phone number are in the Suppliers and Manufacturers section. The first three pads, intended for the general public, are mar-

keted under the Bear-Tex name and are 6″ wide by 9″ long by ⅜″ thick. The first type, green in color, is called a scouring pad. The next, brown in color, is a general-purpose pad. The third type, gray in color, is a hand pad. The fourth variety of pad, actually a disc, is intended for the commercial market. Referred to as scrubbing pads, they are from 13″ to 23″ in diameter and 1″ thick. They are used to remove wax and sealant from floor tile. I am particularly fond of the general-purpose and gray-colored industrial types.

If you choose the furnace filter method, buy the cheapest, largest filters available at your local hardware store. It seems that regardless of size, they're always the same price! Furnace filters of any color will work. I just spray-paint them with a can of brown auto primer before constructing the trees. I strongly recommend using a number of pad types along

with the furnace filters—each yields a slightly different-looking tree, and variety is what we are striving for.

1 If you're modeling a larger fore-ground tree and the base of the trunk will show, look for ¼″ to ⅜″ square or round pine, basswood, or balsa stripwood, which you will whittle to a point with a pocket knife.

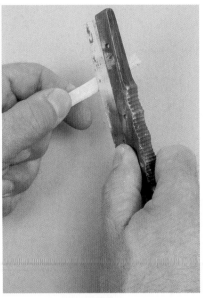

2 Then scribe bark texture into the trunk by drawing a razor saw along the length of its surface.

3 Next drill a no. 55 hole in the base of the trunk

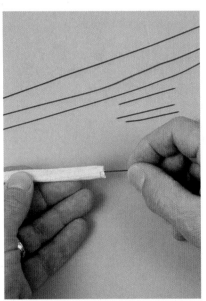

4 Insert a piece of floral wire to aid in holding the tree during assembly and planting.

5 If you're modeling smaller trees, or trees whose branches have grown so low they cover the base of the tree trunk, as evergreens often do, use bamboo skewers that you might find at a local supermarket. Cut them to various lengths, then whittle the base to a point so it too is easy to plant.

6 Stain all the trunks with Minwax Special Walnut stain before assembly. If you are planning to build a large number of trees, it's best to pour the stain into a paint tray and soak the trunks rather than paint them individually. After they have soaked for a few minutes, remove them and wipe them dry with a piece of cotton cloth.

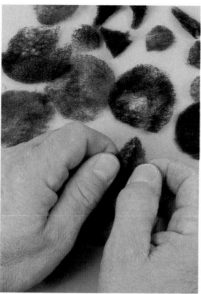

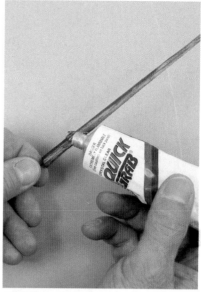

7 Now that you're have finished with the trunks, it's time to prepare the pads for assembly. You can use scissors to cut the pads into circular discs of various diameters, along with a few small triangles for the tops of the trees. (I use my hands to tear the furnace filters.)

8 Now tear each disc into layers, making them as thin in cross section as possible. Pull the triangular pieces apart as well, to give them an airy look.

9 After accumulating a pile of assorted-size discs and tips, start impaling the disks onto the trunks. Working from the top of each tree, apply a small dab of Quick Grab glue before installing each disc.

10 Slide smaller and smaller discs onto the trunk.

11 Finally, top off the discs with a triangular chunk of pad, which forms the top of the tree.

12 What really makes these conifers easy to build is the method I use to create the foliage. Rather than hand-painting the foliage, you can finish off your tree by simply spraying the built-up tree with some Mega Hold hairspray.

13 Then sprinkle on Scenic Express Conifer or Forest Green fine-textured ground foam, alternating coatings of spray and foam until you're happy with the results.

21

Handling Hardwoods

A simple technique for making deciduous trees

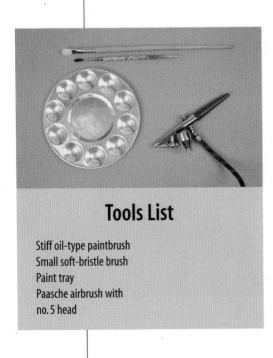

Tools List

Stiff oil-type paintbrush
Small soft-bristle brush
Paint tray
Paasche airbrush with
no. 5 head

S ince my HO scale West Hoosic Division Railroad is modeled after the prototype Boston & Maine and Rutland roads, both of which are located in the Northeastern United States, noted for its heavily wooded countryside, I am always looking for new and better ways to re-create those woodlands in minia-ture. This project covers the materials and construction techniques I have used to create some of my most realistic deciduous trees.

Like conifers, different varieties of hardwood trees have distinct characteristics and shapes. Even though it is not necessary to replicate

Canadian National engine no. 3012 passes the Cobb Farm as it heads along the main line. The hardwood trees beyond the engine were made using the materials and techniques described in this project.

specific types of trees exactly, it does help to recog-nize the features of those common to the area you are modeling. For this reason I suggest, as I did during the conifer project, that you refer to books such as *The Trees of North America* by Alan Mitchell or Harlow and Harrar's *Textbook of Dendrology.*

My three favorite raw materials for constructing

22

Materials List

Raw umber tube acrylic
Burnt umber tube
 acrylic
Assorted gray liquid
 acrylics
Floral tape
Floral wire
Aerosol green paint

Floquil paint:
 Burlington Northern
  Green, 110035
 Coach Green, 110048
 Reefer Yellow,
  110031
 Quick Grab glue

My three favorite raw materials for constructing deciduous trees (from the left): wild spirea, oregano, and commercial peppergrass.

deciduous trees are spirea, oregano, and peppergrass, see the photo above. Spirea grows in abundance at the higher elevations of the Northeast. The plants grow in large clumps (2 to 3 feet in diameter) about 3 to 5 feet high. They can most often be found growing in open, abandoned farm fields before the introduction of first-generation hardwoods.

In its wild state, oregano seems to inhabit the same type of areas as spirea, only at lower elevations. Wild oregano bushes also don't seem to grow as large as spirea. The individual plants will often be found in very small clumps, even single stalks, not over a foot or two in height. Oregano is actually an herb that seems to have spread on its own to open fields in this area. My wife found a large cache of the stuff in an empty lot as we walked along a residential street in the heart of Boston last year. If you prefer growing your own crop of oregano, it is possible. The

local nurseries in my area carry a number of varieties. I have three plants I purchased, all growing like weeds (pardon the pun) in my backyard. The part of the plant that is used to make our miniature trees is really the flower of the bush. It is best picked in mid-fall (about the end of October in this area) when the stalks of the plant have died and are dried out and brown in color.

The last plant I like to use for trees is peppergrass. Accumulating samples of this plant is a lot less adventuresome than the others, since it does not grow wild in this area. It is distributed commercially, however, because of its popularity in dried flower arrangements. For this reason it can be found at almost any well-stocked arts-and-crafts store anywhere in the country. It is available in a number of (dyed) colors. I usually try to buy mine in whatever shade of green is on hand, although since I paint the stuff, it really doesn't matter what color it is.

The other materials I use for my tree-making endeavors are shown in the Materials List. They include, from the local arts and crafts store, floral wrapping tape,

floral wire, tube-type artist's acrylic colors, and plastic bottles of liquid acrylic craft paints. Tube acrylics are of a very thick consistency, much like oil paints, only they are water-soluble. Acrylic craft paints are much more diluted but still thicker than model paint. They too are water soluble. Inexpensive aerosol green paint and a tube of Quick Grab glue come from the local hardware store. Finally, from the hobby shop I acquire the Floquil paints that will form the basis of my various foliage colors. For summer foliage this includes Coach Green, Burlington Northern Green, and Reefer Yellow.

1 Begin by arranging a clump of sprigs (usually four or five) so they resemble the branch structure and crown of a real tree. When you're satisfied with their configuration, wrap two or three layers of floral tape around them tightly.

2 The final step in the assembly is adding a length of floral wire. You'll press it into the bottom of the trunk. The wire will help you hold the tree while you paint it or insert it into the layout. A dab of Quick Grab glue will help the wire stay in place.

3 Once you've made a batch of these little critters (the bigger the batch, the more efficient the operation), spray the foliage with an inexpensive brand of green aerosol paint. Although it's not absolutely necessary, this step will allow you to use less of the more expensive Floquil paint for the final foliage painting.

4 Allow the initial paint application to dry for an hour or two. Then apply acrylics to the trunk of the tree by drawing a stiff artist's brush along the length of the trunk from the crown of the tree to its base.

5 As the acrylic begins to dry, it is possible to pull strands of it out and away from the base to create roots. It's only necessary to perform this step for specimens that will be in the foreground or under close scrutiny. Since the entire tree, including the trunk, will be painted, you can use any color acrylic for this step. I prefer to use raw sienna, burnt umber, or various shades of gray just in case I miss a spot during the final painting.

6 Once the tube acrylics have dried for a few hours, reach for your Floquil foliage colors and airbrush. For summertime foliage use 1 part Coach Green, 1 part Burlington Northern Green, and 1 to 6 parts Reefer Yellow. If you're doing a fall shoot, use Reefer Yellow, Reefer Orange, and Signal Red.

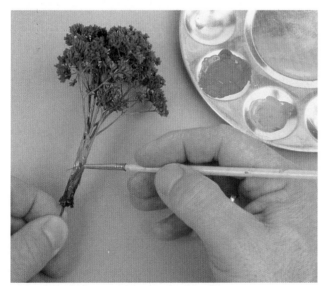

7 The final step in preparing the tree is applying acrylic craft paints (in various shades of gray and brown to represent bark) to the branches and trunk. Squeeze two or three colors into a painting tray and use a soft-bristle brush to apply them to the tree, working down from the branches to the base of the trunk. Try to blend the colors so the finished job is not too monotone.

Super-Duper Trees and More

Real trees in miniature, without much work

Boston & Maine RS-3 no. 1542 crosses the steel deck bridge over Route 20 west of Adams on the B&M main line. The brush in the foreground was made using the materials and techniques described in this project.

Tools List

Scenic Express:
 Concentrated matte
  medium, EXP003
 Spray Mister scenery
  sprayer, EXP023

Self-closing tweezers,
  EXP228-4
Large cooking tin
Clothespins
String

After years of reading, researching, and sharing information with other scenery junkies, I thought I had seen or tried just about all the ways there were to create a good-looking minia-ture hardwood tree for my model railroad.

Then, one day my good friend and fellow modeler Pete Darling happened upon a Scenic Express catalog. Among the products in the catalog was a large assort-ment of different textures and colors of ground foam, Noch Leaf Flake Flocking, and—most important—an item they called the "Super Tree." Pete discovered that, not only did the Scenic Express Super Trees look great, they were also rela-tively easy to build. Most important, he had concluded that the colors used for the foams and flocking marketed by Scenic Express were an exact match to the AMSI ground foams and Floquil

Materials List

Scenic Express:
    Super Tree material,
        EXP214 or EXP215

Noch Elm Leaves,
    N08030

Noch Lime Leaves,
    08020

Noch Birch Leaves,
    08010

paints we had been using for the grass, brush, and tree foliage on my HO scale West Hoosic Division.

The varieties of Scenic Express ground foam that Pete found compatible with our materials are Light Green, Grass Green, Spring Green, Summer Lawn, and Farm Pasture Blend. These can be spread on our miniature hills and dales to replicate either grass or weeds (see the project "Covering Some Ground"). Their Fine Conifer Green works great for foliage on our handmade conifer trees (see "Concocting a Conifer"). Finally, they carry a line of Noch Leaf Flake Flock that, when used on the branch structure of their Super Trees, creates a miniature hardwood tree that's really hard (wood) to beat.

The Super Tree branch and trunk structure is all one piece. Actually, the skeletal component of Super Trees is a wild growth called Filigrane. According to the folks at Scenic Express you can only find this stuff in the high, rocky regions of Scandinavia. If your passport has expired, just order it by the bag from Scenic Express. The trees come in large 12" x 15" plastic bags with enough material to make 50 to 100 trees, depending on their size. You can apply ground foam to the tree structure if you like, but I think the Noch Leaf Flake Flock makes much more realistic leaves. The three varieties that blend best with my other scenery materials are Lime Leaves, Elm Leaves, and Birch Leaves.

1 Begin by stringing a Super Tree "clothesline" of heavy string about 10 feet long across your workspace. Next, fill a basin with diluted matte medium (purchase it pre-diluted or cut the concentrated mix to 1 part medium to 5 parts water). After using an X-acto knife to remove the small leaves attached to the stems, fully immerse some of the trees in the matte medium and let them soak for at least 30 seconds.

2 Remove each tree from the matte medium, using tweezers to grasp it near the center of the trunk. Holding the tree upright, sprinkle on the leaf flocking from above, carefully working your way around the tree.

3 Finally, turn the tree upside down, clip it to the clothesline with a clothespin, remove the tweezers, and let the tree dry upside down. If a tree is particularly crooked, gently clip another clothespin to the top of the tree to pull it straight. Once you have a bunch of the trees hung out to dry, give them all a misting of diluted matte medium in the pump spray bottle to help secure the foliage.

Leaf Me Be

Carpeting the forest floor the natural way

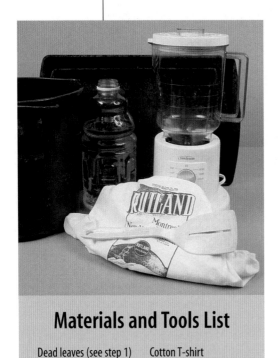

Materials and Tools List

Dead leaves (see step 1)	Cotton T-shirt
Tap water	Cookie sheets
Kitchen sieve	Electric blender
Spatula	Tolerant spouse

If you've ever looked closely at the forests of mother nature you have probably noticed one feature of the forest floor that really stands out—dead leaves. Every year, here in the Northeast, the hardwood trees of the area go into hibernation, dropping their leaves in the process. After losing their color and dropping from the trees, they turn various shades of brown and carpet the forest floor until they decompose and are replaced the following season by a new batch. This constant revitalization creates a brown carpet of decomposing leaves year round.

One day, the members of the Tree Group (actually, three other scenery junkies and I, who would get together in an interactive

A set of B&M F-3s rolls past as farmer Cobb looks on from the seat of his tractor. The leaves along the fence and under the trees to the left of the engine were made by the method described in this project.

support group) were discussing what we could use to create the look of dead leaves on the ground of our miniature woodlands. We decided that nothing could replicate dead leaves better than dead leaves. All we had to do was come up with a way to reduce them in scale. The answer to our dilemma was found at the local K-Mart store. It was an inexpensive blender. Ours was a 6-speed Sunbeam Model 4143 that we paid under $20 for. I'm sure you can find a comparable model from other manufacturers.

1 Begin by raking up a couple of bags of leaves. It's best to do this after a dry spell of weather so the leaves are dry; otherwise, they may rot during storage. If you are going to grind them right away, you don't have to worry about dryness.

2 To grind the leaves, first remove the heavier stems, then place the leaves in the blender, filling it about half way.

3 Add water to the top of the leaves, and do remember to replace the top on the blender.

4 Turn the blender to Frappé (medium/high) for about a minute.

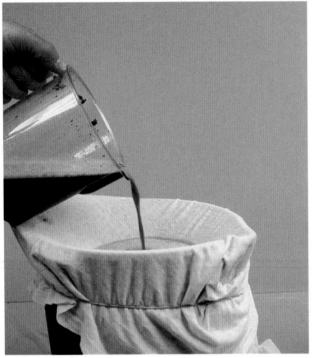

5 Stretch the old cotton T-shirt across the top of a bucket and pour the resulting mess into it.

6 After letting it drain for a few minutes, wrap the shirt around the mix and squeeze out as much water as possible.

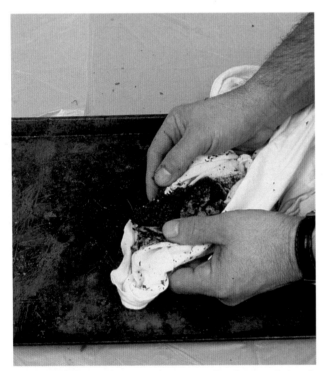

7 Spread the remaining leaves on a cookie sheet and place it in the oven. Set the temperature to 200 degrees (Fahrenheit) and leave the door ajar about 2 or 3 inches. This allows moisture to escape as the leaves are heated.

8 To speed up drying time, use the spatula to turn the leaves occasionally. If you don't want to cook your leaves (or if your wife is by now becoming a bit too hostile because of the disappearance of all her kitchen utensils and her favorite T-shirt dust cloth), you can opt for spreading the leaves out on some newspapers and letting them air-dry.

9 Once the leaves are completely dry, run them through a kitchen sieve or old window screen to filter out the finer-textured material.

10 Hang on to the filtered and unfiltered leaves. As you will see in the following projects, both can be used in making scenery.

Finishing the Forest Scene

Making trees into a forest

Tools List

1"-wide soft-bristle
brush
Artist's spatula
Teaspoon
Awl
Tweezers

Scissors
Pump sprayer for "wet"
water
Pump sprayer for matte
medium

If you have been tackling the projects in this book sequentially, you know how to Cover Some Ground, Leaf Me Be, Concoct a Conifer, Handle a Hardwood, and slap together a Super-Duper Tree. Now it's time to combine all of these techniques and create a finished forest scene.

Besides the materials needed for this project, you will need a supply of "wet" water (tap water with a few drops of dishwashing liquid added) along with an assortment of "handled" hardwoods, "concocted" conifers, and Super-Duper Trees. It usually takes about 30

The motorcar has broken down and the boys are trying to figure out how to get it loaded onto the flatbed. Maybe the fellow from the mill can get some of his co-workers to help out. The woods in the background were created using the materials and methods described in this project.

assorted sizes and types of trees to fill a 1-foot-square area. This will vary according to how thick you want your woods to appear.

Materials List

Pittsburgh Tobacco Brown interior flat latex paint, 7607
Matte medium (If using a concentrate, dilute 1 part medium to 5 parts water.)
Ground Goop mix: 1 cup Celluclay, 1 cup Permascene, 1 cup earth-color latex paint, ⅓ cup white glue, and one capful concentrated Lysol disinfectant

Assorted textures of dirt (see "Covering Some Ground")
Twigs
Coarse- and fine-ground leaves (see "Leaf Me Be")
Small rocks
Assorted textures and colors of ground foam (see "Covering Some Ground" for list)
"Wet" water (tap water with a few drops of dishwashing liquid added)

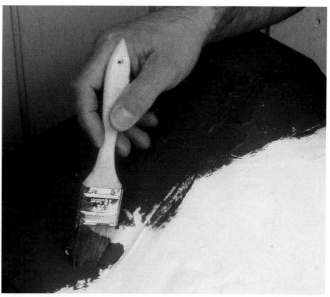

1 Begin by prepainting the scenery base with full-strength earthtone latex house paint.

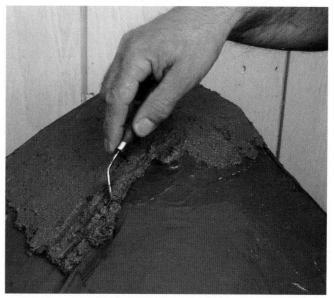

2 Next, use a spatula to spread a ⅛"-thick layer of Ground Goop over an area approximately 1 foot square.

3 Cover the Goop with various textures of sifted dirt.

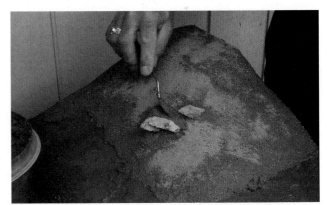

4 Press some larger stones into the Goop, then build up additional Goop around them to make them look as if they're embedded in the soil and jutting out of the hills.

5 Now sprinkle some very coarse dirt around the stone out-croppings to resemble loose gravel that has been worn away and exposed by the elements.

6 Use a spoon to add various textures and colors of ground foam.

7 Randomly place a generous assortment of twigs into the Goop to represent fallen branches and small trees, then add coarse- and fine-ground leaves to the entire scene.

8 Once you're satisfied with the overall effect, spray the entire scene with matte medium until it is thoroughly saturated. You may need to reapply more dirt, foam, and dried leaves to any bare areas that wash away, then lightly re-spray everything with more matte medium.

9 With the groundwork done, it's time to add bushes and trees. While working with Super Trees, I found that their branch structure can also be used to represent brush. You can accumulate brush samples by trimming the individual branches off the stems of the previously prepared Super Trees with a pair of scissors.

10 Jab a hole in the goop with a small awl, then dip the Super Tree branches in white glue and press them into the holes with a pair of tweezers.

11 After adding the brush to the scene, dip the different types and sizes of hardwood and conifer trees into the white glue and press them into the goop at random.

12 Finally, add the Super Tree branches around the perimeter of the woods to represent the secondary growth and brush that thrives in that area and then allow a couple of days for the entire scene to dry.

Light Rock for Your Easy Lifting Pleasure

Making rock outcroppings from Foam Putty

Tools List

Putty knife

Woodland Scenics Foam Knife, ST1433

Soft-bristle brush for removing excess foam cuttings

Assorted small soft-bristle brushes to apply acrylics

Small stiff-bristle brush to apply pastels

For years I've been reading about various ways to replicate rock outcroppings in miniature using different types of plaster. Unfortunately, when you make rock outcroppings for your model railroad with plaster they weigh almost as much as the rocks you're trying to re-create! Well, Woodland Scenics has come to our rescue with a new product they call Foam Putty. This stuff comes in 16-ounce containers and is part of their Subterrain Lightweight Layout System.

Foam Putty looks and handles like spackling compound but weighs about one-third as much. It can be

B&M RS-3 no. 1507 rolls across the Maple Street grade crossing.

used to fill cracks between the Subterrain Styrofoam sheets, build grades for roads, provide smooth subsurfaces for structures, and, most important for us, create rock outcroppings. Fortunately, it is also compatible with other scenery base materials, not just Styrofoam. It can be applied with a putty knife, carved with an X-acto knife (I strongly suggest using a Woodland Scenics Foam Knife), and when dry, colored with the same acrylic colors that we use on plaster rocks.

Materials List

Woodland Scenics	Weber/Costello:
Foam Putty, ST 1447	Hi-Fi Gray pastels,
Raw sienna tube acrylic	145-003
Raw umber tube acrylic	Earth Tone pastels,
Mars black tube acrylic	145-011

1 Start by globbing generous amounts of Foam Putty on your scenic base.

2 After allowing the putty to dry thoroughly (about two days), use the Foam Knife to remove any unnatural-looking formations and carve rock outcroppings into the putty.

3 Remove any trimmed residue with a soft-bristle brush.

4 Squeee about 1 inch of each acrylic color into three paper cups (one color per cup), add about a tablespoon of water to the first two colors and three tablespoons to the last. Begin by applying raw sienna.

5 Next, use a new brush to apply raw umber.

6 Follow with an application of Mars black.

7 Once the initial application is complete, highlight any splotchy colors until you're satisfied with the overall effect. After the acrylics have dried, brush on some assorted colors of Earth Tone and Hi-Fi Gray pastels.

Swamp Thing

Creating miniature
wetlands in four
simple stages

Rocks, Rivers & Ponds

Although commonly seen in nature, swamps and bogs are scenic features that most model railroaders tend to avoid replicating. I have a couple of swamps on my West Hoosic Division, and I think both are pretty good representations of the real thing. Let's follow the four-stage process I use to create my miniature wetlands.

It's a beautiful summer day in 1957 as Rutland RS-3 208 rolls past one of the many swamps along the Ogdensburg Branch of its namesake railroad.

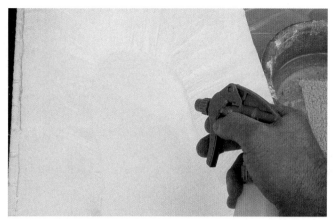

Stage 1: Swamp bottom

1 You'll use two-part epoxy to model your "swamp water." To keep it from eating into the Woodland Scenics subterrain extruded foam base material, first lightly spray the foam with some "wet" water (tap water with a few drops of dishwashing liquid added) before applying the plaster cloth.

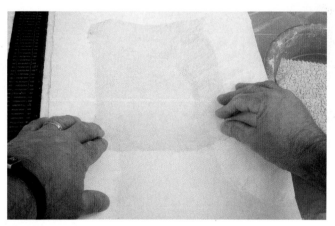

2 Then apply a couple layers of (soaked) plaster gauze around the perimeter and onto the bottom of the swamp area.

3 Use a soft-bristle brush to apply a coating of full-strength earth-color latex paint to the area surrounding the swamp.

Stage 1 Tools List

Scenic Express:
  Spray Mister, EXP023,
    for applying water
Soft-bristle 1"-wide
paintbrush, for latex
paint

Artist's spatula, for
Ground Goop
Stiff-bristle oil paint-
brush, for artist's acrylics

Stage 1 Materials List

Dishpan for water
Raw umber tube acrylics
Burnt umber tube
acrylics
Black tube acrylics
Pittsburgh Tobacco
Brown interior flat latex
wall paint, 7607

Ground Goop (See mix
of ingredients in
"Covering Some
Ground")
Woodland Scenics:
  Plaster cloth, C-1203
  Assorted Subterrain
    foam panels

4 Squeeze out some full-strength raw umber tube acrylics.

5 Use a stiff paintbrush (one made for artist's oil paints) to blend the acrylic and tan latex earth paint to create a murky brown color.

6 Now apply full-strength black tube acrylics to the deepest areas of the swamp.

7 Blend the black with the raw umber to create the illusion of depth to the Envirotex water you'll apply later.

8 After the paint and acrylics dry, apply a layer of Ground Goop mix (see "Covering Some Ground") up to the edge of the swamp.

Stage 2 Tools List

Teaspoon
Awl
Tweezers
Pump-style Mega Hold
hairspray

Scenic Express:
  Spray Mister, EXP023,
    for applying dilute
    matte medium

Stage 2 Materials List

Weld Bond glue
Coarse and fine-textured
ground-up dried leaves
from "Leaf Me Be"
Assorted twigs
Woodland Scenics:
  Polyfiber mesh, 178
  Blended Turf
    Foam, 49
    Flowers, T-48
AMSI:
  Spring Green foam
    (fine), 401

Spring Green foam
  (coarse), 402
Yellow Green foam
  (fine), 411
Yellow Green foam
  (coarse), 412
Grass Green foam
  (fine), 441
Grass Green foam
  (coarse), 442
"Concocted" conifers
"Handled" hardwoods
"Super-Duper" trees

Stage 2: Swamp land and debris

1 After planting various trees in the wooded lot surrounding
the swamp, use a spoon to spread a thick layer of coarse leaf
material onto the swamp base.

2 Next, sprinkle fine-textured dried leaf material around
the shallow wet areas of the swamp. It will represent a
murky residue.

3 Once you're satisfied with the appearance, cover the entire
area with a light spray of diluted matte medium.

4 Since some species of conifer (mainly spruce and hemlock) proliferate around damp areas like swamps, plant some buffing-pad evergreens here and there for effect.

5 Use small chunks of buffing-pad material to create the thick brush found around the perimeter of your swamp.

6 Next, cut small clumps of branches from the stem of the Super Trees and then use an awl to jab a hole in the Ground Goop.

7 Use your tweezers to dip the branches in Weld Bond and plug them into the holes. You can also glue an assortment of dead twigs to the Goop to represent fallen trees and brush trimmed along the right of way.

8 Once everything has dried well, add different textures and colors of AMSI foam foliage.

9 Now sprinkle Woodland Scenics flowers (sparingly) to the surface of the buffing pads applied earlier around the perimeter of the swamp.

10 Finally, use a spritz of hairspray to hold these textures in place.

Stage 3: Swamp grass

Stage 3 Tools List

Tweezers
Scissors

Pump-style Mega Hold
hairspray

Stage 3 Materials List

Weld Bond glue
Assorted brushes (from arts and crafts shop)
Air fern (from craft or flower shop)
Caspia (from craft or flower shop)

Woodland Scenics:
Field grass (medium green), FG-174
Field grass (light green), FG-173
Field grass (harvest gold), FG-172

1 To replicate the tall swamp grass and weeds that grow in the water, start by clumping three varieties (colors) of Woodland Scenics field grass together.

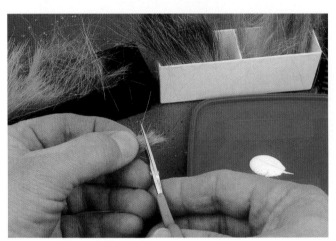

2 Grasp the resulting bunch between your thumb and forefinger, then trim off (square) one end of the grass with a pair of scissors.

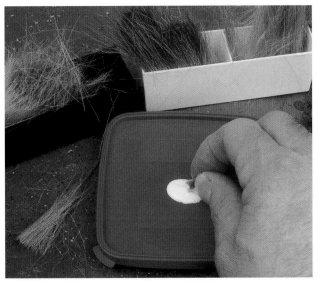

3 Shift the bunch to your other hand, then cut off a grass clump about ¼″ long and dip it in Weld Bond.

4 With the glue-dipped end facing downward, place the clump in position in your swamp.

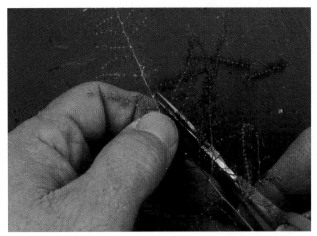

5 Once it's in place, gently tap the top of the grass to spread it apart. You can use the same technique for planting the broom material, but only trim one end of each clump. This gave the broom bushes an uneven top and thus added visual interest.

6 You can also plant individual sprigs of air fern and caspia using a similar technique. Start by using scissors to trim off some small branches.

7 Use tweezers to dip the air fern in Weld Bond and plant it in the swamp among the field and broom grass.

8 Adding a dead tree made from a twig finishes the scene.

Stage 4 Tools List

Craft sticks
Stopwatch or wrist-
watch with second hand
Paper cups

Stage 4 Materials List

Envirotex high-gloss two-part epoxy-resin (from arts and crafts store)
Envirotex mixing instructions:
Use two separate paper coffee cups to perform the process. First fill one cup halfway with liquid resin and the other cup halfway with the hardener. Pour the hardener into the resin and mix them thoroughly with a craft stick while timing the procedure with a stop watch or the second hand on your wrist watch.

Stage 4: Swamp water

1 After thoroughly mixing the Envirotex polymer "swamp water" according to the instructions, carefully pour the resin onto the swamp base. The capillary action of the epoxy causes it to spread among the previously planted weeds and grass.

2 Then gently exhale across the surface of the resin to draw the bubbles to the surface. At 70 degrees and 40 percent humidity, it takes about 72 hours for the epoxy to cure fully.

Down by the Old Mill Stream, Part 1

Adding various bodies of water to your scenery

Tools List

Scissors
Small paint roller and paint pan
Medium-size soft-bristle brush, for applying earthtone paint
Caulk gun

(2) small soft-bristle brushes, for feathering earthtone and black paints along pond edge
Paper cups, for hot liquids
Craft sticks, for stirring two-part epoxy

O ne of the most interesting "real world" scenic features for model railroaders to replicate is water, and in the Northeast water can be found in abundance. In the early to mid-20th century mills and millponds were also plentiful. Millponds were usually created by damming a stream. These ponds served a number of purposes. They supplied water for the manufacturing process, water for fire protection, and, finally, water to turn the turbines that powered the machinery in the mill. Since those mills were more often than not served by railroads, it was a "given"

It's late afternoon, and almost everyone has left, except for the shift supervisor and night watchman at Peerless Tanning Company.

that a number of mills and ponds should be included on my 1950s Boston & Maine model railroad.

For this project, I decided not only to build a mill and pond but also a waterfall flowing over a dam along with a cascading stream. I explained the construction of the scenery base for my millpond and stream in the project "Foaming at the Base," earlier in this book. I am now going to discuss construction of the finished

Materials List

Woodland Scenics:
   Plaster cloth, C1203
   Styrofoam sheets
Pan for water
Pittsburgh:
   Tobacco Brown
      interior flat latex
      paint, 7607
   Semigloss black
      interior paint,
      7757

Latex primer
Dap Dynaflex 230
indoor-outdoor clear
latex sealant
Evergreen Scale Models
clear .010"-thick
styrene, 9006
Envirotex Lite polymer
coating
Styrene cement
Weld Bond glue

1 I decided to have my pond bordered on two sides by woods and on two sides by the large wooden mill (Peerless Leather) and dam.

pond and stream. Since this is a relatively complicated endeavor, I'm going to divide it into two parts. In the first part, I will show you how to create the millpond, install the mill and dam, pour resin pond water, and complete the initial stages of the pond outfall.

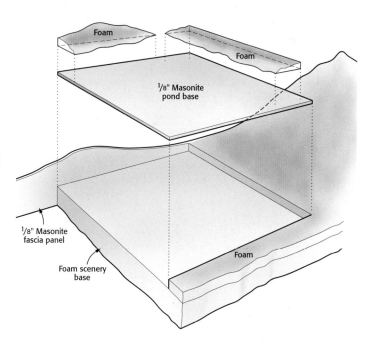

2 In the project "Foaming at the Base," I decided to line the bottom of my pond with ⅛"-thick Masonite to protect the foam panels from the Envirotex water and provide a smooth surface for the bottom of the pond.

49

3 After cutting foam panels to fit around the perimeter of the Masonite, use Weld Bond to glue them in place.

4 Cover these panels with a double layer of Woodland Scenics plaster gauze so that they, too, will be protected from the Envirotex "water."

5 Dip the strips of plaster gauze in water for a few seconds then apply it over the foam panels.

6 Rubbing the surface of the cloth helps to activate the impregnated plaster.

7 Use a small paint roller to first spread latex primer onto the pond base.

8 When the primer coat is dry, use a roller to apply a smooth coat of black paint onto the pond base.

9 Next, using a brush, paint the ground around the pond perimeter and under the mill with earthtone latex paint. Where the hillside met the pond water, I carried the brown out into the pond for about an inch.

10 While waiting for the paint to dry, apply a bead of clear latex caulking around the base of the mill building where it will meet the resin water. This prevents any resin from seeping underneath the building.

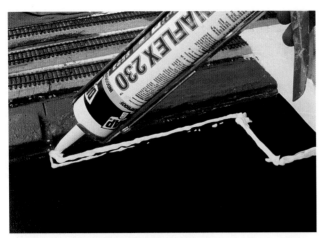

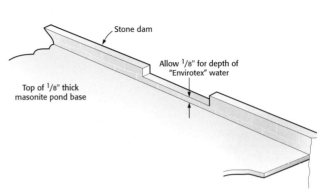

Stone dam

Allow ⅛" for depth of "Envirotex" water

Top of ⅛" thick masonite pond base

11 Apply an additional bead of clear latex caulk onto the Masonite pond base just inside the building walls as an additional barrier.

12 You also want to run a bead of caulk along the upper edge of the dam and place the dam into position so that the spillway is above the surface of the Masonite by ⅛".

13 Place the mill and dam permanently into position.

14 Now apply Ground Goop and various textures of dirt and foam up to the edge of the pond, making sure to fix everything with matte medium. After completing the base scenery, use a soft-bristle brush to apply a generous coating of black paint up to the previously painted earth color.

15 Using a second brush, immediately apply earth-color paint, with the intent of gradually blending the two colors to create a soft-edged transition from one to the other. This gives the illusion that the ground drops off into the depths of the pond.

16 While the earthtone paint is still at hand, apply a coat of color to the base of the streambed that eventually becomes a cascading stream below the pond.

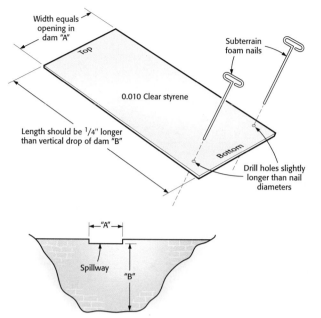

Width equals opening in dam "A"

Top

0.010 Clear styrene

Subterrain foam nails

Length should be ¹/₄" longer than vertical drop of dam "B"

Bottom

Drill holes slightly longer than nail diameters

"A"

Spillway

"B"

18 Test the fit of the styrene piece first.

17 At this point, also cut a piece of .010" styrene as illustrated in the sketch above to serve as a base for the waterfall flowing over the dam.

19 Now you're ready to glue the styrene to the spillway of the dam.

20 Finally, after mixing the two-part Envirotex resin according to instructions (1 part resin to 1 part hardener), pour the resin into the pond until it reaches the top of the outfall.

Down by the Old Mill Stream, Part 2

Adding various bodies of water to your scenery

Tools List

Woodland Scenics:
   Foam Knife, ST1433
   Foam Nails, ST1432
Medium paintbrush, for applying earth-color latex paint
Artist's spatula
Teaspoon
Fine-mesh kitchen sieve
(2) Pump sprayers, for "wet" water and matte medium
	(3) Stiff-bristle brushes, for applying gloss medium and latex caulk
	Wood stirrers, for Envirotex
	"Hot" paper cups, for Envirotex
	Toothpicks, for applying epoxy
	Caulk gun, for applying Dynaflex caulk (not shown)

A s I mentioned in Part 1 of this project, millponds were almost always created by damming an existing stream. For this reason it seemed only logical that I should have some sort of cascading stream leading away from the millpond I built in Part 1. Since I was already using real dirt and small chunks of rocks, in combination with Ground Goop, to make rock outcroppings in my scenery (see the project "Finishing the Forest Scene"), I felt that using real

Rutland Engine no. 403 crosses a deck girder bridge over the Sacco River on its way to Bellows Falls, Vermont. The river was created using the materials and techniques described in this project.

rocks for my streambed wouldn't be that difficult. After all, hand-carved or molded plaster rocks weigh almost as much as the real thing, and you have the additional challenge of coloring plaster to match the surrounding terrain. By using

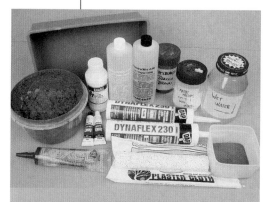

Materials List

Woodland Scenics plaster (cloth) gauze, C1203

Brown latex paint, such as Pittsburgh Tobacco Brown interior flat latex paint, 7607

Ground Goop mix: 1 cup Permascene, 1 cup Celluclay, 1 cup earth-color latex paint (Pittsburgh Tobacco Brown), 1/3 cup white glue, 1 capful of concentrated liquid Lysol, and water.

"Wet" water (tap water with a few drops of dishwashing liquid added)

Scenic Express matte medium, EXP003 (If it's concentrated, mix 5 parts water to 1 part medium.)

Dark-colored dirt

Five-minute epoxy

DAP Dynaflex:
    230 clear latex caulk, 43471
    230 white latex caulk, 43468

Lexel clear "Super Elastic" sealant

Liquitex medium-viscosity acrylic gloss medium, 5008

Envirotex "pour-on" high-gloss finish, 2032

Shallow pan

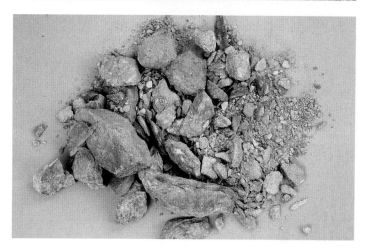

real rocks in combination with talus from the same source, it would be possible to have everything blend together naturally.

I found the rocks for my stream jutting out of a hillside along a county road about 20 miles from my house. In the photo at top right, yours truly fills a 5-gallon bucket with the raw materials for his streambed. If you look closely, you can see how rain and erosion have caused the rock outcropping at the upper left of the photo to disintegrate and wash down the slope below. Remember, you want not only larger rocks but also the talus or eroded material (see photo above). I would guess that a 5-gallon bucket would yield enough rocks and talus for an HO scale streambed about 200 (scale) feet long by 40 (scale) feet wide.

The author collects rocks and talus for the "Old Mill Stream."

The raw materials for the streambed.

1 Start developing the streambed by placing rocks into position at the waterfalls and various locations along the edge of the stream.

2 Remove the rocks and seal the river bed with plaster gauze.

3 After the gauze dries, paint over it with Pittsburgh Tobacco Brown latex paint.

4 Apply "Ground Goop" with an artist's spatula over the streambed and about 3 or 4 inches up the sides of the surrounding hillsides.

5 Press larger rocks into the wet "Goop."

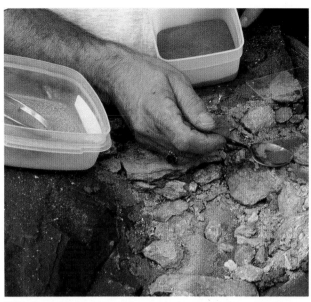

6 Now use a spoon to spread smaller stones and rubble around larger rocks at the sides of the stream and at the various waterfalls.

7 After sifting some of the eroded material through a fine kitchen sieve, use a spoon to spread the resulting dirt over the bed of the stream. Add the darker dirt to enhance the illusion of water depth.

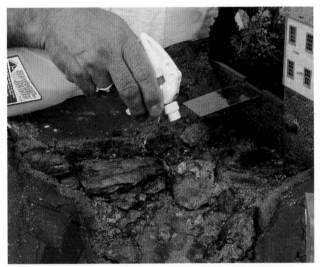

8 Once everything is in place, use a pump spray to apply "wet" water over the entire area.

9 While the scene is still wet, thoroughly saturate the entire area with matte medium.

10 After allowing everything to dry for 2 to 3 days, pin the styrene outfall (from the pond built in Part 1) to the streambed with Foam Nails and glue it in place with 5-minute epoxy. Remove the nails after the epoxy dries.

11 Work the ground cover and trees up to the edge of the stream, then use a stiff-bristle brush and long vertical strokes to apply a thin layer of latex caulk to the surface of the .010 plastic outfall. This gives the illusion that the water is streaming out of the pond and down to the riverbed.

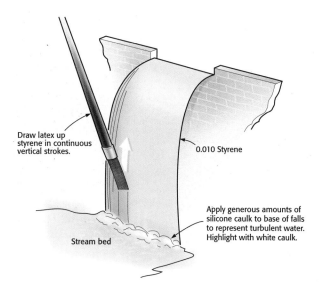

Draw latex up styrene in continuous vertical strokes.

0.010 Styrene

Apply generous amounts of silicone caulk to base of falls to represent turbulent water. Highlight with white caulk.

Stream bed

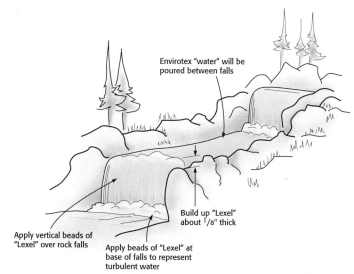

Envirotex "water" will be poured between falls

Build up "Lexel" about 1/8" thick

Apply vertical beads of "Lexel" over rock falls

Apply beads of "Lexel" at base of falls to represent turbulent water

12 You'll also want to apply a generous amount of clear latex caulk at the base of the falls to represent the turbulence that would occur there. Be sure to use latex caulk for these steps, because silicone-based caulks would attack the styrene.

13 Use a product called Lexel to create the water cascading over the rocks in the stream and serve as a dam for the Envirotex. You'll need about four applications of Lexel to make the falls thick enough to hold back the Envirotex.

14 Apply beads of Lexel over the rock faces to represent the foam created by the turbulence of the water.

15 Once the clear latex caulk on the outfall and the Lexel dry, dab a small amount of white latex caulk at the base of the falls.

16 Latex caulk dries to a flat finish, so you may want to brush-paint Acrylic Gloss Medium over the latex caulk on the outfall to provide a glossy "wet" appearance.

17 After waiting a day or two for everything to dry thoroughly, you're ready to mix and pour Envirotex into the river bed.

18 Applying Acrylic Gloss Medium with a stiff-bristle brush over the Envirotex in a fan-like swirling motion helps to create the impression of flowing water.

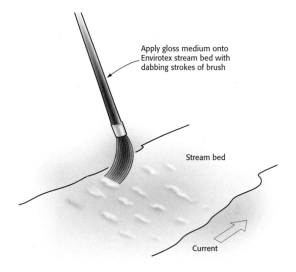

Apply gloss medium onto Envirotex stream bed with dabbing strokes of brush

Stream bed

Current

19 Since the water in the streambed should be moving, I used Acrylic Gloss medium to create the waves caused by the flow of the water in the stream. I applied it with a stiff-bristle brush in a fan-like swirling motion.

Fence Me In

Stone wall boundaries along the right-of-way

Whenever I travel through the country-side, especially here in the Northeast, I notice that stone walls are one of the most common sights along the roadways and rail-road rights-of-way. That is because it was a common practice for farmers, whether they raised cattle or grew crops, to clear the stones from their fields and pile them along the perimeter of each cultivated or grazed area. This practice accomplished two things. It cleared the fields and helped to delineate their boundaries. With the introduction of barbed wire, farmers added wire fences along their stone walls to further restrict access to and egress from their fields.

I found the raw material for my walls along the side

A local farmer takes time out from repairing his fences to watch B&M engine no. 1542 roll by with a freight in tow.

of a local dirt road. I just scraped up a bit of the stuff and ran it through a kitchen sieve until I was left with scale-size wall stones (photo below left). I also found my fenceposts on field trips. They are actually sections of small twigs broken from brush growing on the road-side. Just as the farmers did, I had to turn to a commercial supplier for my barbed wire. It is produced in sizes that will work with both HO and O scale by Scale Link Company of Great Britain.

Use a kitchen sieve to separate the wall stones from the unwanted dirt and gravel.

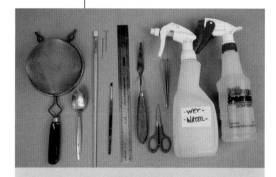

Tools List

Kitchen sieve
Artist's spatula
(2) pump sprayers, one for '"wet" water, one for matte medium diluted 5 to 1
Small scissors
Scale ruler

Foam Nail (or large pin)
Tweezers
Small soft-bristle paint-brush for Floquil paint
Small stiff (oil-type) paintbrush for dry pigments

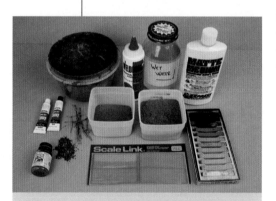

Materials List

Stones
Sticks (fenceposts)
Scale Link Company barbed wire:
    For HO scale use F62
    For O scale use 32F1
Weld Bond glue
Five-minute epoxy
Ground Goop mix: 1 cup Permascene, 1 cup Celluclay, 1 cup earth-color latex paint (Pittsburgh Tobacco Brown), ½ cup white glue, 1 capful of

concentrated liquid Lysol, and water.
Assortment of dirt and ground foam
"Wet" water
Floquil Rail Brown paint, 110007
Scenic Express Concentrated Scenery Cement matte medium, EXP003
Weber/Costello Alpha Color Hi-Fi Grays (dry pigments)

1 Decide where you want to locate your wall, then begin by spreading out a thin layer of Ground Goop (see the project "Covering Some Ground" for mix instructions).

2 Next, sprinkle on assorted textures of real dirt.

3 Also sprinkle in some ground foam.

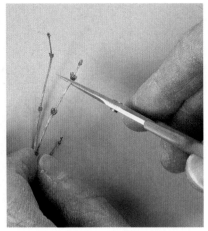

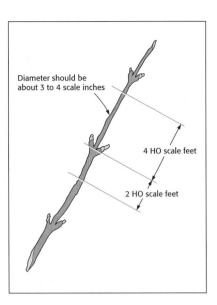

Diameter should be about 3 to 4 scale inches

4 HO scale feet

2 HO scale feet

4 Using pump sprayers, apply "wet" water followed by diluted matte medium.

5 Trim off the top of the fencepost (twig) 4 scale feet above a set of buds.

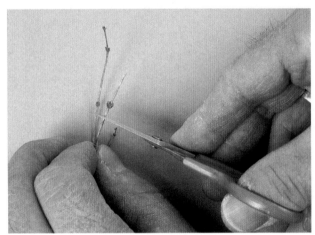

6 Trim off the base of the fencepost (twig) 2 scale feet below the set of buds.

7 To prepare for installation, use a scale rule to measure the distance between posts (approximately 8½ scale feet), and a foam nail to punch a hole in the scenery.

8 After dipping the base of the fencepost in Weld Bond glue, install it using tweezers.

9 Build the wall stone by stone. Dip a stone in Weld Bond glue and place it in position (larger specimens at the bottom) with tweezers.

10 Apply a generous coating of matte medium to "fix" everything in place, and let it dry completely.

11 Use a foam nail to apply a dab of 5-minute epoxy or Super Glue (two posts at a time) to attach the barbed wire to the fenceposts.

12 Press the barbed wire into the epoxy with your fingers (ouch!) or a pair of tweezers.

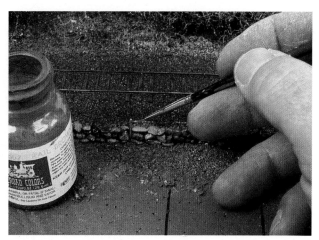

13 After the glue dries, paint the wire Floquil Rail Brown.

14 Matte medium gives the stones a slightly glossy appearance. Brush on some Hi-Fi grays to tone down the sheen.

Tilling the Soil

Create a farm field along the railroad right-of-way

Considering this country's agricultural history, logic would dictate that a tilled farm field should be a part of almost any American modeler's railroad. Before explaining how I created the tilled field in this project, I turned to a close friend who spent his childhood living and working on a farm here in upstate New York: Rich

Cobb. By providing an understanding of the basic steps necessary to prepare a field for farming, planting as well as harvesting techniques used by farmers over the years, he helped me better understand the effect I wanted to create.

I decided it was time to create my miniature farm field. Since I had recently become the proud owner of a GHQ 1953 International Harvester tractor and "Little Gem" 3-bottom (blade) plow, I decided to create a field with the plowing in progress. Before I could do so, I had to

It's getting late in the day as Farmer Cobb takes a break from plowing to watch Rutland Engine no. 403 pass in the distance.

come up with a tool that would replicate the look of plowed soil. Scrounging through my desk, I found a pair of pinking shears. I noticed that the distance between the points on the blade was a little over 12 (HO) scale inches. This very closely matched the distance between the blades of my Little Gem. I cut a piece of .020" sheet styrene about an inch wide and 2 inches long, then cut one end off with the pinking shears. This would be my plowing template (left).

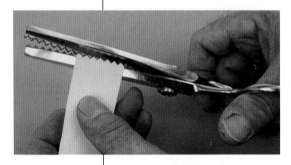

Cut the plowing template from a sheet of .020 styrene.

A Lesson in Farming

By Rich Cobb

Planting

Up until the late 1960s the accepted practice in farming was to plow the land prior to planting a crop. This not only turned the grass and weeds under, but also mixed in any manure that might have been spread on the field. Flat fields were usually plowed in the longest dimension of the field, with furrows perpendicular at the ends. Hillsides were plowed across the hill to prevent erosion. Plowing left furrows in the field about 12 inches apart, and large clumps of soil. The next step was to use a disc harrow. This was a series of sharp wheels (disks) that broke up the lumps and smoothed out the field (Woodland Scenics makes a tractor/disc harrow set—item 207). An alternative was a spiked-tooth harrow, which was a frame with rows of spikes that broke up the lumps. This was sometimes used after disking if a particularly level surface was desired, such as for a hay field.

Farmers in the Northeast planted a variety of grasses: hay, alfalfa, clover, timothy, orchard grass, and others. Crops included corn, oats, wheat, and in recent years, soybeans.

Corn was planted with a corn planter. In early years a two-row planter was used that required an operator on it. Rows were planted about 30 inches apart so that the tractor and cultivator could be used for weed control. In the 1960s and '70s the development of selective herbicides made the use of cultivators unnecessary. A corn planter consisted of a wedge-type shoe for each row that opened the soil. A container above the shoe fed in small amounts of fertilizer, and a second container held the corn seed, which was selected by a notched wheel that dropped a seed about every two inches. Behind the shoe was a flat wheel that packed the soil down on top of the seed and fertilizer (Woodland Scenics tractor/planter set—item 208).

Oats and wheat were planted with a grain drill—a large rectangular box with wheels at either end and shoes spaced every couple inches apart, which opened the soil for the seed.

Hay crops were planted with a seeder—a hand-cranked mechanism with a small canvas bag for seed that was hung over the shoulder as a farmer walked up and down the field. Later years saw the development of tractor-pulled seeders. Following planting, the field was usually gone over with a roller to press the seed into the ground.

Hay would probably be harvested for several years from a field. The field would then be used for a pasture or plowed under for a grain crop. The same would be true for grain crops. After several years a different crop would be planted.

Harvesting

Hay was cut with a mower and then allowed to dry several days before being raked into windrows with a hay rake. In the early days the hay would be pitched into wagons with pitchforks. Later a mechanical hay loader was developed that was pulled behind the wagon. The farmer would stand on the wagon and stack the hay as it came off the loader. The 1940s saw the development of the tractor-drawn hay balers. Early ones had 4-cylinder air-cooled Wisconsin motors. Later models were powered by a take-off shaft from the tractor. Bales were either rectangular in shape, tied with twine or wire, or round. The round ones withstood rain better, as only the outer layer would spoil, but the process was a lot slower. In either case, the farmer tried to get the hay into the barn before it got wet. In early years the bales were dropped on the ground and loaded by hand onto the wagon. Later years saw the development of chutes to carry the hay from the back of the baler to the wagon. This still required either someone to stack the bales on the wagon, or "kickers"—mechanisms that threw the bales into a wagon with sides and a back on it.

At the barn, loose hay on the wagon was picked up by a hay fork, which pulled the hay up to the peak of the barn. There it moved on a track to the desired mow, where it was dropped. Bales were unloaded by hand, or else an elevator carried the bales at an angle up into the mow, where someone stacked them.

Corn in the early years was also cut by hand, stacked on a wagon, and taken to the silo, where a stationary blower chopped up the corn and blew it up a pipe into the top of the silo. The next development was a harvester that cut one or two rows of corn at a time and tied the stalks in bundles, which still had to be moved by hand to the silo. In the 1940s corn choppers were developed. Either self-propelled or run by a tractor, the chopper cut up the corn in the field and blew it into a wagon, which was then unloaded into the blower at the silo. The wagons had movable chains on the floor or movable gates that moved the corn into the blower. The 1940s also saw the development of the corn picker—a tractor-powered device that picked the ears off the corn stalks and loaded them in a wagon for feed grain. Later the combine was developed, which removed the ears from the stalks and then removed the individual kernels of corn from the cobs.

Grains were harvested with threshing machines—originally large machinery that was parked near the barn. The wheat or oats were brought to it from the field. Later, tractor-powered machines were made that could go into the field. Still later, combines took over the job. The straw from either crop was usually baled up to be used as bedding for the livestock.

Tools List

Artist's spatula
(2) pump sprayers, one
for "wet" water and one
for matte medium
Spoon, for applying dirt

Vacuum cleaner
Tweezers
Kitchen sieves
Plastic tilling template

Materials List

Ground Goop mix: 1 cup
Permascene, 1 cup
Celluclay, 1 cup earth-
color latex paint
(Pittsburgh Tobacco
Brown), ½ cup white
glue, 1 capful of concen-
trated liquid Lysol, and
water.
Fine sifted dark dirt

Scenic Express Farm
Pasture Blend Flock &
Turf, EXP886B, with
business-card magnet
applied to bottle cap
(see text)
Matte medium
"Wet" water (water with
a drop or two of liquid
dishwashing detergent
added)
Masking tape

1 Start by using an artist s spatula to spread an ⅛"-thick layer of Ground Goop over the scenery base.

2 Give the surface of the Goop a light misting of wet water to make it more workable.

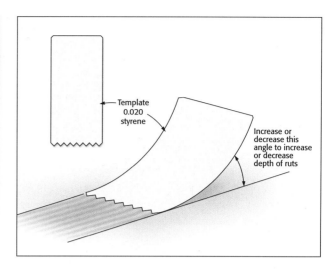

Template
0.020
styrene

Increase or
decrease this
angle to increase
or decrease
depth of ruts

3 Lightly pull the styrene template across the surface of the Goop to create the furrows made by the plow.

4 After making the furrows, use a teaspoon to sprinkle fine dirt over the surface of the Goop.

5 Vacuum up any excess dirt so it does not fill in the ruts in the Goop.

6 Now use a pump sprayer to lightly apply a mist of matte medium to "fix" the dirt.

7 Once you decide where you want to locate the tractor and plow, you can press-fit the tractor into the Ground Goop.

8 The plow is very fragile, so use a pair of tweezers to make depressions in the Goop that simulate the grooves made by plow blades.

9 Test the fit of the plow into the grooves, but don't affix the equipment until everything is dry.

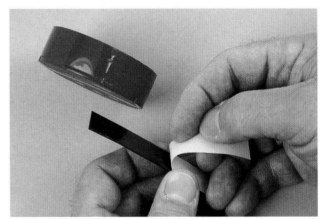

10 While waiting for the field to dry, you can prepare to apply static-charged Scenic Express flock. (It stands upright on the surface.) First use scissors to cut a strip of flexible magnet material. I used business card magnetic backing pads I purchased from a local Mail 'n More store. They are 2" x 3½" pads about 1/32" thick with a self-stick backing on one side.

11 Peel away the paper backing from the magnet.

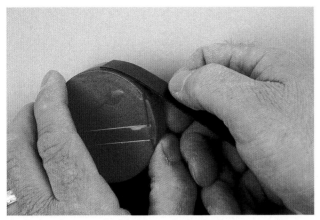

12 Stick the magnet to the side of the bottle cap.

13 Now that the Goop and dirt are dry, use masking tape to cover the area of the field you don't want textured with grass.

14 Use a pump sprayer to mist the exposed ground with matte medium.

15 While the ground is still wet, vigorously shake the container of flock before you sprinkle the Flock & Turf texture over the prepared area. Don't reinstall the farm equipment until everything dries thoroughly.

Do It in Dirt

Build a dirt road for your model railroad

There was a time when the highways and byways of this country were all dirt. Before the advent of the automobile, wagons and stage coaches, then railroads and trolleys provided the most efficient means of transportation. Paved rural roads were not a high priority. City streets were often paved with brick or stones, but once a person ventured beyond these urban areas the streets reverted to dirt. Although the internal combustion engine has managed to change all that, if one travels far enough off the beaten paths (interstates) of 21st-century America, it is still possible to find dirt roads in abundance.

Creating a miniature dirt road is not difficult, but by utilizing the inherent qualities of Ground Goop I found that it was possible to enhance the appearance of my dirt roads. Let me explain. When autos or trucks roll along a dirt road they inevitably create two ruts along the length of its surface. The displaced dirt from these ruts piles up in the middle and along both sides of the roadway. When the base for a dirt road is made from Ground Goop, it is easy to replicate this feature.

Ed Stiles and Rich Cobb, two local farm boys, shoot the breeze as the shadows of the late day sun stretch across one of the many farm roads that criss-cross the countryside in Berkshire County.

Roads

Tools List

Fine and medium
kitchen sieves, for sifting
dirt
Artist's spatula, for
spreading Goop
Teaspoon, for spreading
dirt

(2) pump-type spray
bottles, one for "wet"
water and one for matte
medium

Materials List

Ground Goop mix: 1 cup
Celluclay, 1 cup
Permascene, 1 cup
earth-colored latex
paint such as Pittsburgh
Tobacco Brown, ½ cup
white glue, one capful
concentrated Lysol dis-
infectant, and water.
Woodland Scenics Green
Blended Turf, 49

Fine- and medium-
textured sifted dirt
"Wet" water (tap water
with two or three drops
of dishwashing liquid
added)
Matte medium (if a con-
centrate, use 1 part
matte medium to 5
parts tap water)

1 Begin by wetting the area where you will spread the Goop with some "wet" water.

2 Use a spatula to spread the Ground Goop about ⅛" thick along the path of your road.

3 Press the spatula into the surface of the Goop to create two parallel indentations (ruts) that run the length of the road surface.

4 Soften the edges of the ruts with the spatula.

5 Use a spoon to spread fine dirt over the road's surface.

6 Then use the spoon to spread coarser dirt along the edge of the road. It will represent displaced loose gravel.

7 Sprinkle Woodland Scenics Green Blended Turf (used to represent grass and weeds) along the edges and between the two ruts to blend the road with the surrounding areas of vegetation.

8 Lightly apply a mist of "wet" water over the entire roadway.

9 Spray on a generous coating of matte medium to fix all of the various materials in place.

Rocky Road Adventure

Build a crushed stone roadway for your model railroad

Today, as in the fifties, while most major state and interstate highways in the country are paved with macadam or concrete, many smaller municipalities can't afford the expense of well-paved roads. For that reason, it is still possible to find town and county roads that are either unpaved or covered with crushed stone. After watching the crews from the local highway department cover my street with crushed stone, I decided to come up with a way to replicate that type of roadway on my HO scale layout.

While rummaging through my scenery materials, I found a bag of Highball Products N scale Dark Gray Ballast. About the same time, I had hired a local mason to install a brick walk to my front porch. He was using a product called stone dust, rather than mortar, to fill the gaps between the bricks. After taking a closer look at the stone dust, I decided to use it, in combination with the ballast, to create a crushed-stone road.

Rutland RS-1 no. 403 crosses Maple Street as it heads south on the Rutland, Vermont– Chatham, New York, branch.

Tools List

Artist's spatula
Teaspoon
Fine kitchen sieve

Scale Scenics Micro
Mesh brass screen,
652-3501
Pump sprayers

Materials List

Ground Goop mix: 1 cup
Celluclay, 1 cup
Permascene, 1 cup
Tobacco Brown latex
paint, ⅓ cup white glue,
and I capful Lysol con-
centrated disinfectant.
See "Covering Some
Ground" for materials
list and manufacturers.
Stone dust, available at
any well-stocked stone
and gravel company
Concentrated matte
medium diluted 5 to 1
with water

Highball Products N
scale Fine Dark Gray
Ballast, 122
"Wet" water (tap water
with a few drops of
dishwashing liquid
added).
Ground-up leaves (see
"Leaf Me Be")
Assorted textures of dirt
Assorted textures of
ground foam
Scenic Express Summer
Lawn Blend flocking,
EXP881B

1 Begin by using a spatula to spread a thin layer of Ground Goop onto the road base and surrounding area.

2 Next, use a fine kitchen sieve to sprinkle the ballast over the Goop.

3 After thoroughly covering the Goop with gravel, work the surrounding scenery materials up to the edge of the road.

4 Once everything is in place, use a pump sprayer to mist "wet" water onto the road surface and adjacent scenery materials.

5 Next, use a pump sprayer to apply a generous amount of diluted matte medium.

6 Use a spoon to fill any irregularities or low spots in the dampened road surface with additional ballast.

7 Now you can apply a layer of filtered stone dust (use the same fine sieve you used for the ballast) to the wet road surface. Place the dust on a piece of very fine brass screening and scrape a spoon across the material, forcing it through the screen and onto the road surface.

8 Finally, after everything dries thoroughly, use your finger to smooth the surface of traffic lanes to simulate where the vehicle tires have pulverized the stone and softened the texture of the surface.

Concrete Streets from Styrene Sheets

Build a concrete roadway for your model railroad

Although many of the major roadways across America today are macadam, back in the 1940's and '50s most newer city streets and higher-traffic rural roads were built using concrete. Because of a highway relocation in the '60s, one such stretch of state road just a few miles from my house remained very much as it looked in the '50s. Since my HO scale Boston & Maine West Hoosic Division Railroad was set in a '40s to '50s timeframe, I thought a similar concrete thoroughfare would be appropriate for my layout. After spending an afternoon measuring and photograph-

ing the prototype roadway (opposite page, center) I came up with the following information. A typical concrete rural roadway would be about 21 feet wide. It would be poured in sections. Each section or slab was poured 10½ feet wide (to the center line of the road) and 25 feet long.

After some experimentation, I decided to use Evergreen Scale Models .020″-thick styrene plastic sheets to replicate the concrete pavement (see sketch on the opposite page, bottom). Also depicted in the sketch are .020″ styrene reinforcement panels that would be glued to the underside of

Boston & Maine RS-3 no. 1542 crosses Maple Street on its way north as traffic rolls along State Highway 2.

adjacent roadway sections. These panels should be about an inch wide.

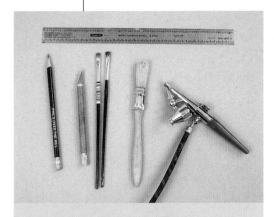

Tools List

No. 2 lead pencil
X-acto knife with no. 11 blade
(2) small stiff-bristle oil-painting brushes for applying pastels

Small soft-bristle brush for applying white glue
Paasche airbrush with no. 3 head
Scale ruler

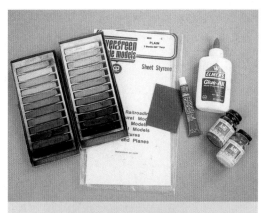

Materials List

Weber/Costello:
  Hi-Fi Grays, 45-003
  Earth Tones, 145-011
Evergreen Scale Models
.020" plain sheet
styrene, 9020
400-grit emery cloth, available from hardware and auto supply stores

Tube-type polystyrene cement
Elmer's white glue
Floquil paint:
  Reefer White, 10011
  Concrete, 110082

This prototype photo of old State Route 9 north of Saratoga Springs, New York, was taken in the early 1970s.

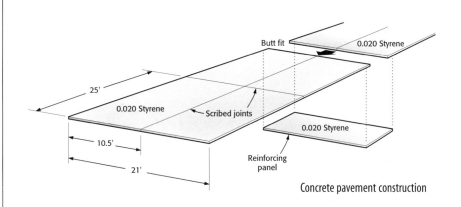

Concrete pavement construction

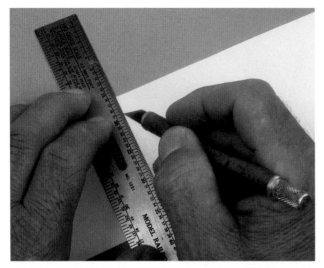

1 Begin by drawing the roadway separations on the styrene. Then, using two or three light passes, scribe the division lines between sections with the back of the no. 11 blade.

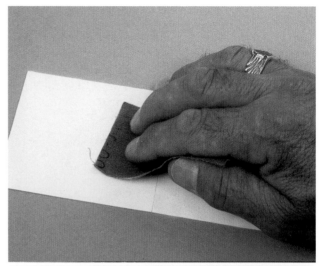

2 Remove any excess styrene shavings by sanding the surface with 400-grit emery cloth.

3 After test-fitting each section, but before assembly, spray the road panels with a mix of 3 parts Floquil Reefer White to 1 part Floquil Concrete. Allow the paint to dry, then add reinforcing strips to the bottom of the adjoining road panels

4 Apply full-strength white glue to the scenery base before installing the panels.

5 Now apply more white glue to the bottom of panels and place them into position.

6 Work the scenery materials up to the edge of the pavement. Then use a stiff-bristle brush to apply earthtones and gray pastels to weather the surface.

7 Finally, use a soft cotton cloth to blend the pastels into the surface of the road.

Flanger Lift Flags

A trackside detail you can model

One trackside detail found on prototype railroads in the northern areas of the country, but seldom seen on model railroads, is the flanger lift flag. The flags I have seen here in the Northeast are usually sheet steel panels mounted on a length of angle iron or pipe. They are painted either black or yellow. Placed strategically along the right-of-way, they warn the crew of a snow-removal train to lift the flanger of their snowplow so it doesn't strike an obstacle. (The flanger is the part of the plow that removes the snow from between the rails.) You would see lift flags on the approaches to bridges, turnouts, and highway crossings or at any location where an obstruction between the rails might cause the flanger to foul. The sketch on the opposite page at top right depicts the dimensions and configuration of a typical flanger lift flag.

I positioned my flags about 40 to 80 scale feet from an obstacle and on the engineer's (right) side of the track. For more information on flanger lift flags, refer to Kalmbach's how-to book *Trackwork and Lineside Detail for Your Model Railroad.*

Rutland engine 403 rolls along the Corkscrew Division of its namesake railroad. The crewman enjoys a smoke as the engine heads east into the warm morning sun.

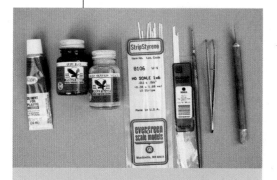

Tools & Materials List

Testors plastic cement
Polly Scale paint:
  Grimy Black, 414137
  Reefer Yellow,
    414122
(1) package Evergreen
Models strip styrene
.011" x .066", 8106 W-4

(1) package Plastruct
styrene round rod
.030", MR-30 (90853)
or K&S 1/32"-diameter
brass wire
Soft-bristle paintbrush
Tweezers
X-acto knife with no. 11
blade

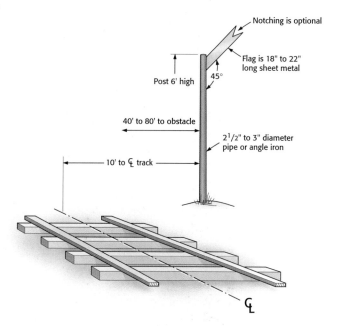

Notching is optional

Flag is 18" to 22"
long sheet metal

45°

Post 6' high

40' to 80' to obstacle

2 1/2" to 3" diameter
pipe or angle iron

10' to ₵ track

₵L

Flanger lift flag prototype dimensions and configuration

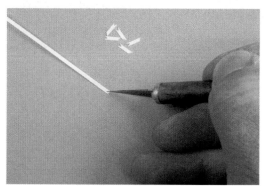

1 Begin by cutting the flag out of a piece of .010 x .060 Evergreen strip styrene with a new no. 11 X-acto knifeblade.

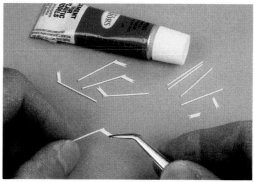

2 Cut a short length of Plastruct .030 styrene round rod for a post. Then place a dab of plastic cement on the flag to affix it to the side of the post, using tweezers.

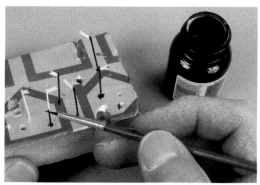

3 Once the glue has set, brush-paint the post Polly Scale Grimy Black.

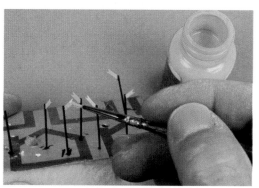

4 Finish the project by brush-painting the flag Reefer Yellow.

Lay It on the Line

Telegraph lines along the railroad right-of-way

One detail that really adds visual interest to a period layout is the presence of line poles along the miniature railroad's right-of-way. Unfortunately, too many model railroaders leave these poles shiny plastic and devoid of wire, detracting from the realism they are attempting to create. I have found that, with Rix poles, button thread, and a little extra work, I could greatly improve the appearance of the telegraph lines on my HO scale West Hoosic Division.

In my area, railroad telegraph poles seem to have been shorter than utility company powerline poles. They would usually be from 15 to 25 feet tall. The number of crossarms per pole ranged from one to as many as five or six, depending on the location (main line or branch line). Pole insulators would be glass, ceramic, and even rubber. Glass insulators were either clear or various shades of green. Ceramic insulators were brown or white, and rubber insulators were flat black. Telegraph (and telephone) lines were usually copper. Since copper oxidizes and turns green in time, I used light green thread to replicate this.

There is an excellent article on line poles along with other helpful articles on line-

Rutland RS-3 no. 208 rolls along one of the road's branch lines with a local freight in tow.

side details in the Kalmbach book *Trackwork and Lineside Detail for Your Model Railroad.*

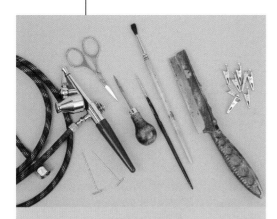

Tools List

Razor saw
X-acto knife with no. 11 blade
Spring clips
Foam Nails
Scissors
Awl
Airbrush

Fine-tipped brush, for applying Floquil paints
Medium-tipped brush, for applying the Poly Scale paint or the India ink–alcohol mix

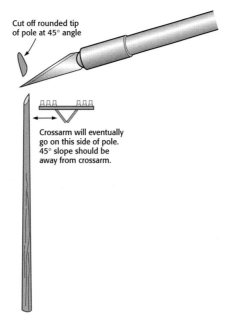

Cut off rounded tip of pole at 45° angle

Crossarm will eventually go on this side of pole. 45° slope should be away from crossarm.

1 Begin by removing the Rix poles from their sprues. Either 30 or 40-foot poles will do—just cut them to the desired length. Trim their tops to a 45-degree angle with an X-acto knife

Materials List

Rix Railroad telephone poles:
    30 and 40-foot poles, 628-30
    72 crossarms, 628-31
Floquil paint:
    Earth, F110081
    Burlington Northern Green, F110035
    Crystal Cote, F110004
    Rail Brown, F110007
Polly Scale paint:
    Roof Brown, 414275

Testors plastic cement
Elmer's Glue All (white glue)
Weld Bond glue
Fine (100-grit) sandpaper
India ink–rubbing alcohol mix, 1 teaspoon ink to 1 pint rubbing alcohol
Light green no. 50 mercerized sewing thread

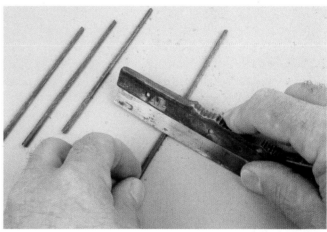

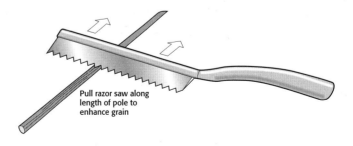

Pull razor saw along length of pole to enhance grain

2 Next, draw a razor saw along the length of the plastic pole to create wood grain.

3 Use fine (100-grit) sandpaper to remove any excess plastic shavings.

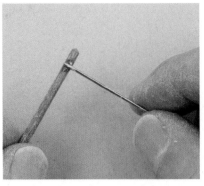
4 After you've determined the number of insulators you want per pole, shorten the crossarms using an X-acto knife. Before installing the crossarm, apply a dab of plastic cement to the pole.

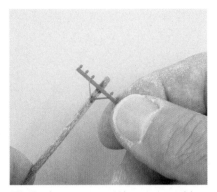
5 Fix the crossarm–V brace assembly into position.

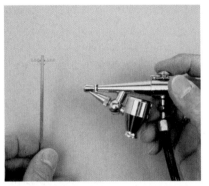
6 When the glue has set, airbrush the entire pole assembly with Floquil Earth paint.

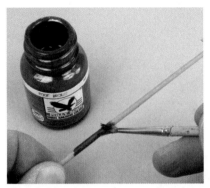
7 Brush-paint the bottom of the pole Poly Scale Roof Brown to re-create the effect of age and weather

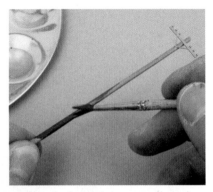
8 Dip the brush in water and, working your way up the pole, blend the brown into the previously applied earth color.

9 After the brown coloring dries, apply a coating of India ink–alcohol mix to the entire pole assembly.

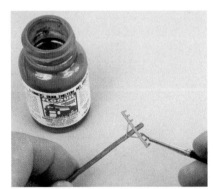
10 Paint the insulators Floquil Burlington Northern Green.

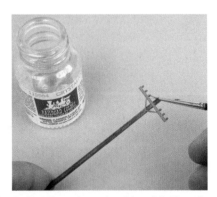
11 When the paint dries, dab Floquil Crystal Clear onto each of the insulators to create a "glassy" appearance.

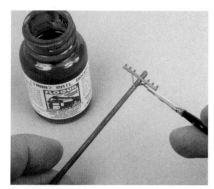

12 Now paint the V braces Floquil Rail Brown to finish the poles.

13 To install the poles (positioned 10 scale feet off the center of the track and 80 feet apart), use a small awl to jab a hole in the Styrofoam scenery base.

14 Dip the pole into Weld Bond glue and place it into the hole.

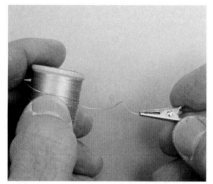

15 Add the wire (thread) after the glue has set. First, attach a spring clip to one end of the thread.

16 Lay the thread over the first pole next to an insulator.

17 After stretching the thread from pole to pole, attach another spring clip to the opposite end of the thread to keep the line taut.

18 Use a Woodland Scenics Foam Nail to apply a small dab of white glue on each thread where it came in contact with an insulator. Note: If a damaged line needs to be repaired, you can dissolve white glue by applying a dab of water to it.

19 Finally, when the glue dries, trim excess thread from the crossarms using a pair of scissors.

Making the Grade

Create a safe place for roadways and railways to intersect

Grade crossings have always been a common sight on both prototype and model American railroads. On my West Hoosic Division the wood plank crossing protected by crossbucks has been one of the most realistic and easiest to build.

As you assemble your own grade crossing, be sure to keep the following points in mind. You'll want to use an NMRA track gauge to be certain that the flanges of a railcar's wheels will pass freely between the inside edges of the rails and the planking of your crossing. Also, be careful that the height of the planks is a scale 2″ to 3″ below the rail height. Otherwise, the glad hands or airhoses on your locomotives and rolling stock could catch on the ends of any offending planks.

It's a slow order as Rutland engine no. 208 crosses Post Road on the Chatham Branch.

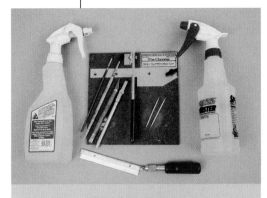

Tools List

Razor saw
Northwest Shortline
Chopper
X-acto knife with no. 11
and no. 17 blade

Toothpicks
(2) small soft-bristle
brushes
(2) pump sprayers

Materials List

Kappler HO scale 4 x 8
lumber, 340
Duco cement
Five-minute epoxy
Ballast
Creative Model
Associates crossbucks,
1009
Rail sections
Floquil Reefer White
paint, 11011

Poly Scale Engine Black
paint, 414290
India ink—rubbing
alcohol mix, 1 teaspoon
ink to 1 pint alcohol
"Wet" water
Diluted matte medium,
5 parts water to 1 part
matte medium
Weld Bond glue

1 Begin by using a small soft-bristle brush to spread ballast under the area you'll cover with planking.

2 Apply "wet" water, then diluted matte medium with a pump sprayer.

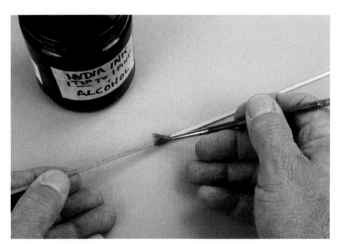

3 Brush on a mix of India ink and alcohol mix to stain the HO scale 4 x 8-foot stripwood planks. The mix should contain 1 teaspoon ink to 1 pint rubbing alcohol.

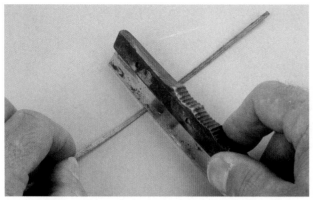

4 Pull a razor saw along the length of the plank to distress the surface and create wood grain.

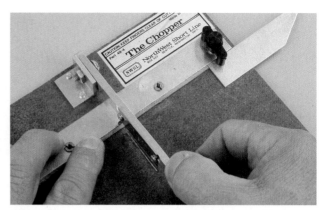

5 Cut planks to the measured length with a razor blade or a Northwest Shortline Chopper, as shown here.

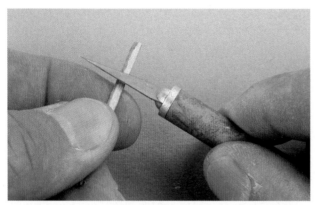

6 Bevel the edge of planks that will be adjacent to the outside of the rail with an X-acto knife.

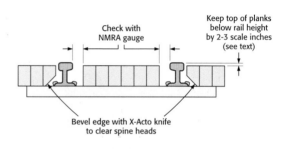

Check with NMRA gauge

Keep top of planks below rail height by 2-3 scale inches (see text)

Bevel edge with X-Acto knife to clear spine heads

Grade crossing dimensions and configuration

7 Glue the planks in position (directly to the ties of this Code 55 trackage). Use Duco cement, which is butyl acetate and acetone-based, to avoid warping the thin pieces of basswood.

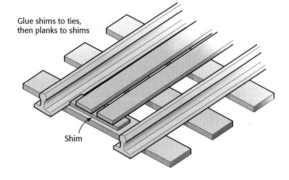

Glue shims to ties, then planks to shims

Shim

Code 83 or 100 rail may require planking of larger vertical dimension; alternatively, you could use wood shims on top of the existing ties.

8 Once the planks are set into position, apply road material—dirt in this example—up to the planks and glue it in place

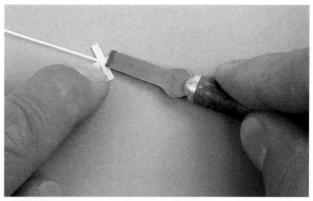

9 Now it's time to add Creative Model Associates crossbucks to protect the crossing. You can use the supplied posts or make your own out of discarded rail by using a no. 17 X-acto knifeblade to cut two pieces of Code 55 rail to length.

10 Apply 5-minute epoxy to the posts with a toothpick.

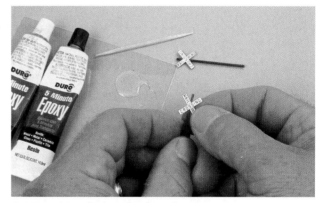

11 Position the crossbuck on the post.

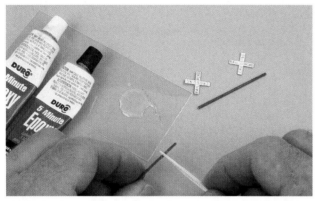

12 Brush-paint the top of the posts Floquil Reefer White to match the crossbucks and the remaining third Polly Scale Engine Black.

13 Finally, apply a dab of Weld Bond to the bottom of the crossbuck assemblies and place them in position 10 scale feet off the center line of the track.

Details Make a Difference

The finishing touch for your model railroad scenery

No matter how well done your basic scenery is, adding those small "real world" details will always make it look even better. Twenty years ago, when I first started construction of my HO scale West Hoosic Division, it was necessary to scratchbuild many of those smaller detail items. Recently, while browsing around my local hobby shop, I realized that things have changed for the better. Of the items they stocked, the products of two suppliers looked particularly interesting. To use along the railroad right-of-way, Creative Model Associates produces some very nice pre-painted

styrene trackside details, including crossing signs, milepost markers, and whistle post signs. To detail my roadways, I chose some of Blair Line's vast assortment of .010 styrene highway signs. I decided to try their traffic signs, highway route markers, street signs, and vintage road signs.

While I was impressed with the Blair Line signs, I noticed that the only materials they supplied for posts were short lengths of either square basswood or round styrene rod. Both seemed rather heavy in cross section. I also felt it would be too repetitive to use only two types of posts for the

We are looking northwest up Route 2 as Rutland engine no. 208 approaches Post Road grade crossing on its trip south from the railroad's namesake city.

various signs. I decided to substitute a variety of styrene shapes for posts. I opted for .030″ round rod, .040″ triangular rod, .030″ square rod, and ¾″ styrene angle. The sketch shows the type of post I used for the various signs along with the colors I painted them.

One other detail I decided to replicate was the wooden guardposts often seen along the highways of the fifties. I used three different materials

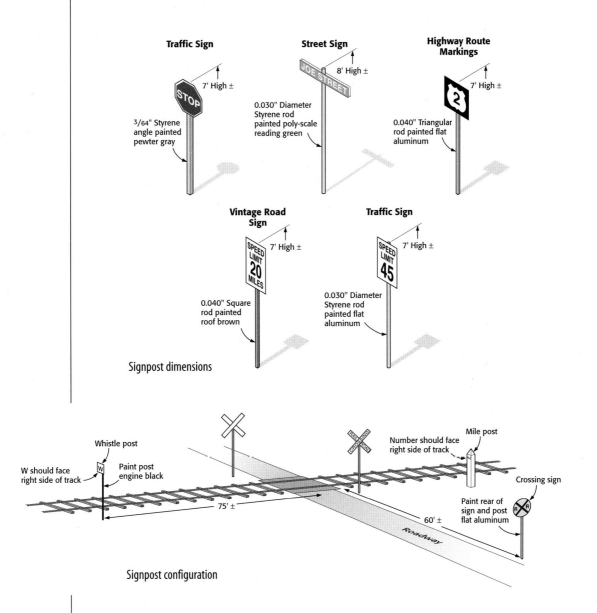

Traffic Sign

7' High ±

STOP

3/64" Styrene angle painted pewter gray

Street Sign

8' High ±

JOE STREET

0.030" Diameter Styrene rod painted poly-scale reading green

Highway Route Markings

7' High ±

2

0.040" Triangular rod painted flat aluminum

Vintage Road Sign

7' High ±

SPEED LIMIT 20 MILES

0.040" Square rod painted roof brown

Traffic Sign

7' High ±

SPEED LIMIT 45

0.030" Diameter Styrene rod painted flat aluminum

Signpost dimensions

Whistle post

W should face right side of track

Paint post engine black

W

75' ±

Number should face right side of track

Mile post

Crossing sign

Paint rear of sign and post flat aluminum

60' ±

Roadway

Signpost configuration

for this: 1/16" round styrene, .060" square styrene, and small lengths of twigs.

Preparation of the signs was simple. I painted the Creative Model Associates yellow railroad crossing signposts Poly Scale Flat Aluminum and the whistle signposts Poly Scale Engine Black. Since their mileposts had two sets of numbers on two separate faces and I could not find that style of post in any of my Northeastern railroad prototype photos, I scraped one set of numbers off with a no. 11 X-acto knife blade and installed the post with the

remaining numbers facing the right side of the track (see sketch).

The Blair Line signs are printed on a sheet of .010" styrene. After cutting out each sign with a small pair of sewing scissors, I used styrene cement to attach each sign to its post. I painted the backs of the signs Poly Scale Old Aluminum. I then painted the posts various colors with Poly Scale paints (see the top diagram on this page). After a light dusting of pastels to soften the intensity of the colors the signs were ready for installation.

Since I had three types of roads on my layout—concrete, crushed stone, and dirt—I decided they would represent state, county, and town roads, respectively. I decided to use 1/16" round styrene rod to create round guardrails for the state roads and .060" square styrene rod for square guardrails for the county roads. Both these types would be painted white and black. The round guardrails on my dirt town roads are simply small sections of twigs cut to length and left unpainted.

To get a better grasp of the impact these small

details have on a scene, let's take a look at the photos. In the lead photo we have a State Route sign in the right foreground. Opposite it on the left is the back of a stop sign, to warn traffic on the dirt secondary road. Across the dirt road we have a street sign indicating that this is, in fact, Post Road. Just to the left of the street sign, along the right-of-way, is a whistle post informing the engineer that he must sound the horn for the upcoming crossing. To the left of the whistle post, a

crossbuck mounted on some old rail protects the grade crossing (see the project "Making the Grade").

In the top photo on this page we have swung the camera further to the left and can see, across the dirt road from the truck, the low-budget, unpainted, guard rails the town has installed along with an old (vintage) speed limit sign. Note how the sign is more rusted and weathered in appearance than the route number sign in the first photo. This effect was created by brushing

Shifting to the left, we see Rutland RS-3 no. 208 at the grade crossing on Post Road.

The intersection of Maple Street and Route 2, looking southwest. Rutland RS-1 no. 403 is at the Maple Street grade crossing.

rust-colored dry pigments on the face of the sign.

In the third photo (second from the top on this page) we have the intersection of the crushed stone county road and the concrete state road. Note the better-main-

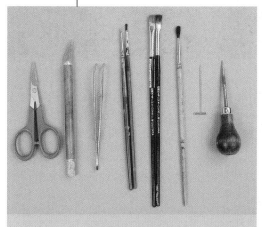

Tools List

Small sewing scissors
X-acto knife with no. 11 blade
Tweezers
Small soft-bristle brushes, for painting posts
Stiff-bristle oil-paint brushes, for applying pastels

Medium-size soft-bristle brush, for applying India ink mix
Woodland Scenics Foam Nail, for punching holes in scenery before installing smaller details.
Awl, for punching holes in scenery before installing larger details.

Materials List

Twigs
Evergreen Scale Models:
  $\frac{1}{16}$"-diameter styrene rod, 222
  .060" square styrene rod, 153
Plastruct:
  .030" styrene round rod, 90853
  .030" styrene square rod, MS-30
  .040" triangle rod, MRT-40
  $\frac{3}{64}$" styrene angle, 90501
Creative Model Associates:
  Crossing signs, 1022
  Whistle posts, 1026
  Mileposts, 1011
Blair Line:
  Highway route markers, 108
  Traffic signs, 102

Traffic signs, 103
Street signs, 109
Vintage road signs, 142
Weber/Costello:
  Hi Fi Gray pastels, 145-003
  Earth Tone pastels, 145-011
Elmer's white glue
Plastruct Bondene plastic solvent cement
India ink–rubbing alcohol mix, 1 teaspoon ink to 1 pint alcohol
Poly Scale paints:
  Reefer Gray, 414116
  Flat Aluminum, 414299
  Roof Brown, 414275
  Engine Black, 414290
  Reading Green, 414376

tained painted guardposts along the state road—the round ones in the left foreground—and the square posts just to the left of the locomotive along the county road. I created these by leaving the tops of the posts raw white plastic and painting the bottoms black. I then gave them a wash of India ink and alcohol to mute the colors. In the middle foreground the street sign lets you know that this is Maple Street, while beyond the crossing there is a 35 mph speed limit sign. On the far

right, along the railroad right-of way, a concrete milepost indicates to the engineer of locomotive no. 403 that he is 41 miles from the beginning of this branch of the railroad.

These are details we always see in period prototype photos but seldom find on the average model railroad. Thanks to manufacturers like Creative Model Associates and Blair Line, we now have an easy and inexpensive way to remedy that situation.

For more information on mileposts, whistle posts, and

a number of other lineside details pick up a copy of Kalmbach's book *Trackwork and Lineside Detail for Your Model Railroad.* Both Creative Model Associates and Blair Line offer other trackside and roadside details. Blair Line has a myriad of signs, posters, and billboards covering from the turn of the 20th century to the present day.

Suppliers and Manufacturers

Activa Products
P.O. Box 1296
700 S. Garrett
Marshall, TX 75670
(903) 938-2224,
(800) 255-1910
www.activa-products.com

Alder Models (Farm Silo)
P.O. Box 1537
Deep River, Ontario,
Canada K0J 1P0
(613) 584-3149
www.magma.ca/~alder
E-mail:
aldermodels@intranet.ca

AMSI
P.O. Box 750638
Petaluma, CA 94975
(707) 763-6000
www.AMSI-minilandscaping.com
E-mail: macamsi@svn.net

Blair Line
P.O. Box 1136
Carthage, MO 64836
(417) 359-8300
www.blairline.com

Creative Model Associates
P.O. Box 39
Plainview, NY 11803-0039
(516) 755-3308
E-mail:dtichy@optonline.net

CS Designs, Inc.
(Scalecrete)
P.O. Box 149
Valparaiso, IN 46385
(219) 464-9463,
(800) 326-7087
E-mail:
csdesign@netnitco.net

Grandt Line Products
1040 B Shary Court
Concord, CA 94518
(925) 671-0143
E-mail: Grandt@pacbell.net

GHQ (farm equipment)
28100 Woodside Road
Shorewood, MN 55331
(612) 374-2693
www.ghqmodels.com

Homabed
California Roadbed
P.O. Box 970
French Camp, CA 95231
(209) 234-6486
Fax: (209) 234-6487
www.calroadbed.com
E-mail:
calroadbed@yahoo.com

Micro Engineering
1120 Eagle Road
Fenton, MO 63026
(800) 462-6975

New Era Products
New Era Plant Clinic
Clinton Nursery Products
Clinton, CT 06413

NJ International
P.O. Box 99
East Norwich, NY 11732
(516) 922-0010
Fax: (516) 922-1564

Norton Company
(polishing pads)
2770 West Washington St.
Stephenville, TX 76401
(800) 331-3604
www.nortonabrasives.com

O&W Shops (custom kit
and scratchbuiding)
109 Cayuga St.
Clyde, NY 14433
(315) 923-9289
E-mail:
richinny@hotmail.com

Precision Laser Craft
(self stick shingles)
32 Beekman Drive
Agawam, MA 01001
(413) 572-0510
Fax: (413) 562-3265
http://members.aol.com/prelasr/index.html
E-mail: prelasr@aol.com

Scale Link Company
Rear of Talbot Hotel
Blandford Road
Iwerne Minster
Dorset, DT11 8QN
United Kingdom
(0044) 1747-811817
www.scalelink.co.uk

Scenic Express
1001 Lowry Ave.
Jeannette, PA 15644-2671
(724) 527-7479
www.scenicexpress.com

Tony's Train Xchange
Pinewood Plaza
57 River Road, Box 1023
Essex Jct., VT 05452
(800) 978-3472
Fax: (802) 878-5550
E-mail: info@tonystrains.com

Woodland Scenics
P.O. Box 98
101 East Valley Drive
Linn Creek, MO 65052
(573) 346-5555
www.woodlandscenics.com
E-mail:
sales@woodlandscenics.com